Revisit, Reflect, Retell

Strategies for Improving Reading Comprehension

LINDA HOYT

HEINEMANN
Portsmouth, NH

To Steve, Brenden, Megan, and Kyle

For your belief in me, your patience,

and your love . . .

Thank you.

Heinemann
A division of Reed Elsevier Inc.
361 Hanover Street
Portsmouth, NH 03801–3912
http://www.heinemann.com

Offices and agents throughout the world

© 1999 by Linda Hoyt

Library of Congress Cataloging-in-Publication Data
Hoyt, Linda.
    Revisit, reflect, retell : strategies for improving reading
comprehension / Linda Hoyt.
        p. cm.
    Includes bibliographical references (p. 193).
    ISBN 0–325–00071–9
    1. Reading (Elementary). 2. Reading comprehension. 3. Reflection
(Philosophy). 4. Children—Books and reading. 5. Education,
Elementary—Activity programs. I. Title.
LB1573.H69   1999
372.4—dc21   98–29644
                                                                              CIP

Editor: Lois Bridges
Production: Elizabeth Valway
Interior design: Joni Doherty
Manufacturing: Louise Richardson

Printed in the United States of America on acid-free paper
08 07 06 05 04 VP 14 15 16 17 18

Contents

Prologue

. . . .

One of the greatest joys in my life is the sense of contentment I feel when I finish an enjoyable story. I sometimes mourn the ending of the story and wish for the characters and the story to live on. Yet I savor the sense of completion that comes with the ending of a story well told. At such moments, I find myself holding on to the story. I roll it around in my thoughts and reflect back on especially meaningful moments and images. As I move back into the rhythms of my own life, the story sometimes goes with me, drifting in and out of my thoughts.

I have never once felt the urge to snatch up glue and scissors to create a diorama or run to my computer to write a concise summary of the plot. Instead, I might tell a good friend about the book or hold the thoughts close as I reflect on the meanings of what I read. When I do attempt to share my thoughts, I find that my emotions and opinions about the story are an inherent part of my communication. A lifeless summary, devoid of my personal response, would somehow devalue my feelings about the experience and rob me of important emotional connections.

One of the greatest gifts we can offer our students is to help them find their own voices as readers as well as writers. The activities that follow are meant as glimmers of possibility and should be thought of as a well from which new ideas might spring. In all cases, the goal is to assist readers in learning how to effectively process information while deepening their personal enjoyment of text and their ability to communicate their thoughts. As you move through the pages of this book, think of yourself as a reader, remembering what responses you most enjoy when finishing a story.

Introduction

. . . .

I remember sitting in class during elementary school, holding my breath, waiting as the teacher's eyes surveyed the
class, wondering if I was to be the unlucky one called on. I remember
feeling helpless. I didn't really care about the story, I just cared about
whether or not I would be the one put on the spot.

Thankfully, few students today are placed in that situation. As
educators, we have come to understand that students must be empow-
ered, not made to feel helpless. Students need to have opportunities to
take responsibility for their own comprehension, not just wait fearfully
to be tested on their knowledge.

Reflection and retelling are ideal vehicles for creating a learning
environment where students delve deeply into their own understanding,
merging their knowledge of the world with the meaning they derived
from what they've read. When these merged understandings are then
communicated through oral, written, or visual systems of communication, the learner is likely to experience deeper levels of understanding
and increased communicative competency.

Guided reflection and retelling have the added bonus of "teaching"
comprehension, while providing a format for "assessing" it. When a
learner retells the content of a reading selection, the reader takes total
responsibility for understanding and then communicating that understanding. The learner is also placed in a situation where he or she must
consciously utilize the elements of story structure to guide the retell
while integrating information from the focus text. Through this process,
an observing teacher has an unrivaled opportunity to understand the

learner. Retellings offer a window into oral and written language proficiency, depth of understanding of text, ability to connect world knowledge to the reading material, understanding of story structure and stylistic devices. This increase in ownership, responsibility (Cambourne 1995), and oral language use provide a learning atmosphere that is significantly more powerful than having a child sit passively and respond to teacher-directed questions.

In my personal experience with guided reflection and retelling, I am continually amazed at how much I learn about the children. As they share their understandings about stories, they often tell about themselves and the personal connections that a reading selection offers them. They offer opinions and justifications for ideas that in a simple written response might have sounded disconnected from the story, but when accompanied by their oral justification are absolutely logical and often very creative.

It has also been my experience that when children are supported in a learning environment that encourages discussion and thoughtful reflection, they begin to expect that level of thinking from themselves. They pick up each text with the expectation that it will make sense and that it is their responsibility as a reader to process the meaning. I find this very exciting; I have worked extensively with challenged learners who unfortunately have often viewed reading as a process of word calling. When we can build a culture where readers expect print to make sense and where they understand that they are responsible for their own learning, everyone is a winner.

One Caution on Guided Reflection and Retelling

Richard Allington and Lucy Calkins suggest that we need to have students engage in fewer formal responses to reading. They fear that students are asked too frequently to write about or create a visual response. If postreading responses become tedious or do not develop oral language and reading proficiency, they may lead to negative attitudes. In many cases, the best and most appropriate response to reading is *more* reading. If we are to assist children in guided reflection and retelling, we must always do it within a frame of authenticity.

It is critical to ask: Is there a reason to believe that this learner *needs* to engage in a structured reflection experience about this text, or is this learner better served by engaging in more reading? If the decision is to guide the learner into reflection and retelling, we must then ask:

1. Is this reflection experience one that will deepen learner understanding and/or increase communicative competence?
2. Does the learner view this task as interesting and meaningful, or busywork?
3. Is there an authentic audience for the reflection?

As in all instructional decisions, we must be sure that the decision to lead children into guided reflection and retelling is a choice that is matched to learner need and interest. It is not the intent of this book to turn reflection into something orderly and mechanical. It is my hope that these activities and forms will always be used in a social context where conversation and interaction are the "test" of understanding. It is even my hope that many forms would never reach the hands of children but rather serve as springboards to reflective experiences that include genuine dialogue and plain paper. I urge you to enjoy!

1

Conversations About Books
Personal and Social Explorations of Meaning

At one time, quiet classrooms were considered the ideal environment for learning. However, as research has demonstrated the social nature of learning, we must remember that it is essential to provide opportunities for children to talk about what they are learning and the strategies they are using for inquiry (Braunger and Lewis 1997). These questions and dialogue need to be genuine acts of communication and not simply a rote reaction to situations controlled by an adult (Peterson and Eeds 1990). Through in-depth, authentic conversations in which children are encouraged to share their opinions and understandings, we can help children to delve more deeply as thinkers, clarify ideas, and verify information.

There is a strong and important link between oral language and reading comprehension (Clay 1972; Wilson and Cleland 1985). Sharing and comparing through the oral mode of communication demands that the learner activate understanding of a story. Together, through conversation, readers can consider the potential meaning of a passage, clarifying their thoughts and reflecting on the processes that help them to create meaning while reading (Hoyt 1992). Through dialogue, readers measure their own understandings against the perceptions of others, consider the quality of their understanding, examine diverse perspectives, and make internal adjustments in their reading. In each exchange, oral language proficiency is bolstered and expanded, elaborated upon and stretched.

Through a long history of working with children who are challenged by learning, I find that these children in particular benefit from conversation. Traditional comprehension questions focus attention on the teacher rather than the text and cast the learner in a passive rather than active role. Cambourne's Conditions of Learning (1985) make it clear that we must increase learner responsibility if we are to increase learning. Conversations and genuine dialogue place responsibility directly in the hands of the learner. Challenged learners who engage regularly in rigorous conversations about texts begin to anticipate engagement in meaningful dialogue and engage in more-intensive monitoring of their own comprehension.

The challenge we face is how to create an environment in which conversations stay focused on the text *and* assist children in connecting their world knowledge with the text being discussed.

Questions for Students to Ask Each Other About Books

What did you notice?

What did you like?

What is your opinion?

What did you wonder?

What does this mean?

What did you learn?

How did it make you feel?

What parts of the story seemed especially important to you?

As you read, were there any places where you thought of yourself, people you know, or experiences you have had?

Were there any parts you especially liked?

What did you read that gave you that idea?

What did you read that makes you think that?

What do you know now that you didn't know before?

Were there any parts you would have changed if you were the author?

What do you think the author did especially well?

What is the strongest literary element?

Questions for Students to Ask Each Other About Being a Reader

How did you function as a learner?

What did you do well?

What did you do to help yourself as a reader?

What strategies did you use most in this book?

- read on to check for meaning
- thought about what made sense
- reread to regain meaning

- used picture clues
- broke unknown words into chunks

What challenged you as a reader?

Are there any adjustments you need to make in your reading?

The Two-Word Strategy

As a listening activity:

1. Read a thought-provoking selection to your students (picture book, newspaper article, passage from a resource book, and so on).

2. After reading, ask students to be *silent* and then to write *only two words* (not in a phrase) that reflect their thinking about the passage. At first it may be helpful to provide a half sheet of paper with a box for each focus word. This helps the students understand that the words do not have to be related or in a phrase.

3. After selecting their words, students turn to someone close to them and read their words, tell why they chose them, and explain how they relate to the story and/or their personal lives.

4. At this point, it works well to create a class list of words that were chosen by various individuals. As each word is added to the list and the rationale for selection is shared, a rich tapestry of understandings about the story begins to surface. Students really enjoy hearing the diverse interpretations and benefit from the wealth of vocabulary that appears on the class list.

The Two-Word Strategy causes students to reflect on the entire selection and relate their own world knowledge to the story *without stress.* "Only two words?" is a common reaction from students. It sounds easy. It is fun, and it causes deep and intensive reflection!

Note: Another benefit is the wait time that is automatically provided as students write their words. This allows all learners, even those most challenged, to have time to collect their thoughts and be ready to engage in the conversation.

As a reading activity:

Follow the steps above but ask the students to read a selection independently, or in groups, then write and share.

Two-Word Strategy

Name of reader _____

Title of book _____

word 1   **word 2**

I chose these words because _____

_____

_____

_____

_____

_____

_____

_____

V.I.P. ("Very Important Points")

Have students cut sticky notes so that there are slim strips of paper extending out from the sticky edge.

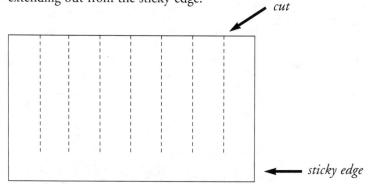

cut

sticky edge

As students read, they can then tear off these pieces of fringe to mark points in the text that they feel are significant. These may be points of interest, points of confusion, points where the student felt a personal connection.

As a postreading activity, students can compare the points they marked and tell why they chose to mark each one. There are no prefabricated questions. Readers simply talk to each other about what they read, using the self-sticking notes as points of reference. It is critical that these VIPs (Very Important Points) be justified in the conversation. As students share their VIPs, they need to make statements such as "I chose to mark this point *because* . . ."

Ideally, the teacher serves as a group member, sharing personal VIPs and the rationale for choosing each one.

To support emergent readers in learning this strategy, I find it helpful to start with predictable books. I read to them while they follow along for a page or two. We then talk about the pictures and the message of the author. Each child is asked to place one VIP on either a part of a picture or a point in the text and then tell why that spot is important. After several experiences, emergent readers find this a very supportive retelling structure, and they are eager to share their VIP observations.

As students gain sophistication with this strategy, they can use it for longer segments of text knowing that the VIP points will help them to reflect and summarize. With some students, I find they enjoy working with one paragraph or one page at a time and then building into longer segments of text.

Evaluative thinking and oral interactions can also be stimulated when students are asked to work in pairs and determine the four or five most important issues in a story or a unit of study. To accomplish this, partners must first reflect on all their VIPs, evaluate the importance of each piece of information, and then collaboratively create a ranking. Older students studying the American Civil War had a fascinating discussion when the partners each presented and attempted to justify their rankings of the war's five most important events. Primary students eagerly talked well into recess time after using this process with *The Velveteen Rabbit*.

Three-Circle Map

Have students draw and/or write in each circle to show what they remember about key elements of the story, then talk to others about their reflections.

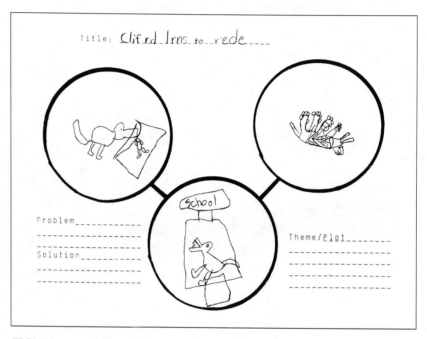

FIGURE 1–1 Clifford learns to read.

Note: This organizer is also a helpful planning device when students are initiating an original piece of writing.

Three-Circle Map

Name of reader: _____

The Story: _____

_____

Problem: _____

_____

The Solution: _____

_____

**What happened first?
(Initiating Event)**

**What happened last?
(Conclusion)**

What was it mostly about?

Novel Reflections

Draw or write three points for each chapter.

Example:
- problem/solution/setting
- 3 key events
- literary devices
- points of tension

Title _____   Reader _____

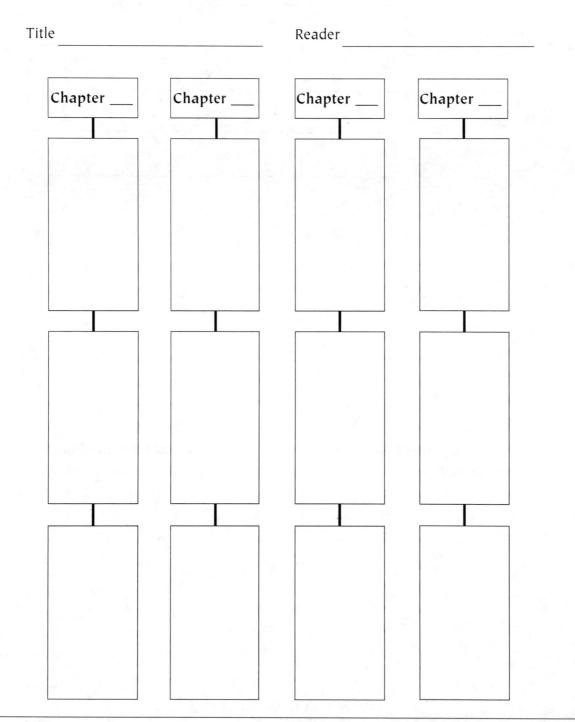

Chapter ___   Chapter ___   Chapter ___   Chapter ___

What Is Important?

The importance of this organizer is not the form itself, but rather the thinking and the conversations it can generate. The goal is to help students understand that all events and characters are not of equal importance in a story. As they begin to evaluate comparative levels of importance, nuances of understanding begin to emerge. The important question at all levels is "Why do you think so?"

In working with emergent readers and writers, I might offer to be their secretary and support their discussion while I draw and write their ideas. As children become more proficient both with writing and with using this organizer, it may turn into shared writing, interactive writing with a group, or an independent activity.

Directions

- Have students reflect on key story elements and list the four believed to be the most critical.
- Rank the elements with #1 being least important to the story.
- List words under each selected element which describe that element *and/or* provide justification for the ranking.

What Is Important?

The Book _____ Date _____

The Reader _____

Focus on: ( )Characters   ( )Events

Least Important	Moderately Important		Most Important
1	2	3	4

Describing words to justify ranking

_____ _____ _____ _____

_____ _____ _____ _____

_____ _____ _____ _____

_____ _____ _____

Tell about your rankings

_____

_____

_____

_____

_____

Backtracking a Story

1. | **Before interacting with a text**
Read the ending of a story to your students, then invite them to discuss or write about the following:

↓

2. | What can you tell about the genre?

Did this remind you of any other stories?

What characters did you learn about in the ending?

Which characters do you think are most important to the story? Why?

What did you notice about the setting?

What predictions could you make about:
    the problem
    the resolution
    key events

↓

3. | **After reading**
Compare: How did the realities of the story compare with our predictions? What did we learn?

Rate yourself: How did you do?

Book Commercials

Commercials and advertisements are a part of nearly every American child's life and can provide the foundation for exciting reflections on favorite stories and units of study.

Samples:

- Are you tired of being hungry? Wondering where your next meal will come from and which day of the week you might find it? At 8:00 P.M. every Monday on Channel 8 you can join *The Very Hungry Caterpillar* for your most challenging food solutions!

- Are you aware that a young boy named Brian recently crash-landed a plane in the wilderness of Canada ALL BY HIMSELF? He survived the crash, then lived on berries and survived incredible acts of nature. To learn more about his incredible adventure, check out the fiction section of the library under *Hatchet* by Gary Paulson.

- Did you know that there is a woman who loves to wash muddy animals? She washes pigs and cows and ducks. She tries to keep them clean—but they keep running back into the mud. Check out *Mrs. Wishy Washy* to find out what happens!

- Write your own!

Book Commercial Form

Name of copywriter for this ad _____ Date _____

Media to be used: Radio, television, magazine ad, newspaper ad, other

The Book to Be Advertised _____

Important Characters _____

Important Points _____

Art for the ad:

My opening question: _____

_____

Details for the middle: _____

_____

An ending that will sell this book! _____

_____

_____

_____

_____

Alphaboxes: A Reflective Strategy

Alphaboxes are a fun and stimulating way to reflect on a story or a unit of study. After reading, students work in pairs or small groups to think of words that reflect important points in the story. They insert their words into the appropriate alphaboxes on the form, making sure they tell how each selected word related to the story. The class then can create a compilation of the most interesting words generated by the groups, making a special point to hear each justification. The result is a lively stretch of vocabulary, a rich network of different perspectives, and a wealth of conversation about the focus story.

Sample for Cinderella

A	B	C	D
	ball	cinders	dirt
		coachman	dainty
		clock	

E	F	G	H
	footmen	glass slipper	
	father		

I	J	K	L
		kind	

M	N	O	P
mean	no one to help		pumpkin

Q	R	S	T
	rags	slipper	
	rats	stepsisters	

U	V	W	XYZ
unfair			

Extension Idea

Students who have watched *Jeopardy* on television enjoy writing questions to go with the focus words. For example: If the students generate RAGS as a word under R, the accompanying question might be What did Cinderella dress in most of the time?

Alphaboxes

The Book _____

The reader(s) _____

A	B	C	D
E	F	G	H
I	J	K	L
M	N	O	P
Q	R	S	T
U	V	W	XYZ

Evaluating Attributes

1. Select an issue that comes out strongly in a story and have the students list ideas related to the topic *before they read.*

2. After the story is shared, have the students evaluate whether or not issues in the story met their expectations. Each point is marked with a plus mark or minus mark as a ranking system.

For example, before introducing *Fly Away Home* by Eve Bunting, which is the story of a young homeless boy and his father living in an airport, students might list what they believe to be the attributes of a home.

Before reading:	After reading:
Attributes of a home	*Present in the story? (+ or −)*
A shelter	+
Is warm	+
Has a bed	−
Is safe	+
Has people who care	−
Is where you eat	+
A place to keep your things	−

As you adjust this format to various titles it might look like the following:

The Three Little Pigs

Attributes of a pig	*Present in the story?*
Likes mud	−
Has tender skin	−
Lives on a farm	−

Hatchet

Attributes of someone who could survive in the woods	*Present in the story?*
Brave	+
Builds shelter	+
Can find food	+
Is smart	+

Attributes of a good conversation	*Present in our discussion*
eye contact	−
turn taking	+
active listening	+

Evaluating Attributes

The Story _____

Signatures of Group Members _____

The attributes of_____   **Present in the story (+ or −)**

_____

_____   _____

_____   _____

_____   _____

_____   _____

_____   _____

_____   _____

_____   _____

_____   _____

_____   _____

Body Puppets

After reading or listening to a story, students determine key characters and then use heavyweight tag paper to draw life-size outlines (from the waist up) of each key character. As they cut out these silhouettes, they also cut out a circle for the face. Clothing and hair can be illustrated for each character.

Volunteers then hold the cutouts in front of their bodies, placing their faces in the holes. Students can then have conversations by taking on the roles of their characters or answering questions from the audience about their character.

FIGURE 1–2 Body puppets

Pick a Part

For this retelling structure, I place strips of paper with the names of story characters in a basket and have students pull out a strip to see which character each person will represent.

1. To prepare for a whole-class activity, I divide the number of key characters into the number of students in the class to decide how many individuals need to represent each character. (For example: A story has five characters and I have twenty-five students in class. I will make five strips for each character in the story so that every student in class will be able to draw a strip from the basket. In this case five students will represent each character.)

2. The students draw their strips from the basket to determine which character they represent. They then return to the text to review and prepare to talk about their character's role in the story.

3. Students meet in "same character" groups to talk about their character's role in the story.

4. The activity moves into a jigsaw format. Groups that have at least one person representing each character are created. These "heterogeneous" groups share about the role of each of their characters in the story, using the text to make points as needed.

Note   If this is a small-group activity, skip step 3 and move directly into the conversation about the characters.

Hot Seat

Hot Seat is an interactive experience that can be used with either literature or content-area studies.

Students are divided into groups with each group becoming an "expert."

- If the topic is literature, then each group could become an expert on a character. In this case they need to be ready to justify that character's behavior in the story. Groups could also become expert on the author's use of characterization, theme, setting, plot, and so forth.

- If the topic is content-area study, expert groups can be formed by dividing the topic into meaningful "subtopics" such as the food, clothing, and housing of the Iroquois Indians.

It is the responsibility of the group to ensure that all members understand the information and are prepared to be questioned.

The Hot Seat Rules

One group is asked to form a semicircle facing the front of the class while audience members take turns posing questions. As each question is asked, the expert group puts their heads together and decides on a *team answer*. (An egg timer is a nice way to limit the time they spend deliberating.) The audience member who asked the question then calls on *one* member of the expert group to verbalize the team answer. Since the group has no idea who will be called upon, they must participate fully while the team answer is selected and then ensure that all members are ready to give the answer.

Students really seem to enjoy the security of the group answer and are challenged by the diversity of this experience. Depending on the text, this could focus on simple recall, in-depth character analysis, or a rich discussion of literary elements. This is a great way to ensure that students of all ability levels learn key information and experience success!

My Character and Me

Invite students to select a character from a story and then compare the character to themselves. In what ways are they alike or different? Do they have similar interests or ways of doing things? If the student had the character's role in the story, would he or she have made any different choices?

A Venn diagram works well for this activity, and students find it especially appealing if you photocopy pictures of the reader and the character and make them available to paste onto the page.

My Character and Me

Name of Character _____

Name of Book _____

Name of child _____

photo of child

photocopy image of character

Word Sorts for Literature

1. *Before reading* provide a word sort such as the one below. To prepare the word sort, select words and phrases from a story. *Be sure they do not see the title of the story or key pictures before they do this.*

Encourage students to tear or cut the words apart so they can be easily moved around. The goal is to arrange the words in an order that supports the telling of a story. Students tell the stories they create using the words and phrases. Support them in including predictions about characters, problem, solution, and so on.

2. *During reading*, stop at a key point. Have the students pull out all words and phrases that have been used up to that point and rapidly retell the story with a partner before making a prediction about how the story might end.

3. *After reading*, have partners scramble the words and phrases and arrange them in an order that supports retelling the story as the author designed it.

Here is a sample word sort using the book *The Piggybook*, by Anthony Brown.

Words and Phrases to put in boxes for a sample word sort

dirty dishes	unmade beds	fix the car
leave home	note on the mantle	cook dinner
wash the clothes	pigs	root around
family jobs cooperation	lonely	

Non-Fiction Note: A meaningful pre-reading variation is to have students sort the words into categories which seem meaningful, tell why they organized their words in this way, then make predictions.

Word Sort

Maybe

Provide the students with a statement that is controversial. Their task is to come up with a balance of reasons (pro and con) for why this statement may or may not be true.

Example #1: *Cinderella's fairy godmother should have given her more time to enjoy her beautiful dress and fancy carriage.*

Agree:	Disagree:
She spent too long in rags.	The story would have turned out very differently if she hadn't had to run from the ball.

Example #2: *Little Red Riding Hood's mother shouldn't have sent her to grandmother's house by herself.*

Maybe

Controversial statement about a book, a character, or a current event.

Agree   Disagree

_____   _____

_____   _____

_____   _____

_____   _____

_____   _____

_____   _____

_____   _____

_____   _____

_____   _____

Group Members _____

_____

_____

Get Real

Good story writers often want their characters to have traits that resemble people in the real world. Your job is to select a character from your story and consider how realistic that character may be. Review your story and select quotes that show whether or not the character is realistic.

Book _____   Character _____

Quote #1. _____

_____

_____

I selected this quote because _____

_____

Quote #2. _____

_____

_____

I selected this quote because _____

Quote #3. _____

_____

_____

I selected this quote because _____

_____

Say Something

When readers are always given a set of questions to answer or discussion starters to stimulate conversation, they can become dependent on such structures or—worse yet—develop the notion that conversations about reading are for the teacher rather than for the readers. Say Something is designed to build the expectation that readers talk to each other about their reading, but what they talk about is up to them. They may choose to respond with a prediction, with a thought about how the text relates to a personal experience, or with an opinion.

I find that in the beginning, this works best as a partner activity.

The Process

1. Students meet with a partner. Each partner should have a copy of the same reading material. You might consider using narratives, magazines, news articles, and so on.

2. The partners make an agreement about how they will proceed with their reading. They might choose to read chorally, trade off by paragraphs, or read silently to a chosen stopping point. When they reach the stopping point, each partner needs to Say Something about the reading.

3. Partners return to Step 2 and select another stopping point before reading on.

An Alternative

Once students learn the process and become comfortable with the expectation that everyone needs to Say Something, they can try this in a group of three or four. As the group size is enlarged, it is very important to ensure that:

- The readers select a method that keeps everyone reading most of the time. They could choose silent reading or unison reading. They might choose readers theater. They could even try trading paragraphs, but here it would be important to have multiple voices reading each part so that tangled readers don't establish ineffective models of reading and the listeners don't have long to wait for their turn. The goal is to read, so strategies that keep readers actively engaged with print rather than spending time as listeners need to be emphasized.

- With a larger group, I have found it helpful to have a structure

Adapted from *Creating Classrooms for Authors,* by Short, Harste, with Burke, Heinemann (1988)

to ensure that everyone Says Something. A cooperative learning technique that works very well is having students put their pencils in the center of the table after they contribute a thought. They cannot talk again until all pencils are on the table. This technique builds the expectation that everyone will need to contribute to the conversation and ensures that strongly verbal learners do not overly dominate the discussion.

Have a Book Party

Book parties can occur within a classroom, as an activity between two classrooms, or as a parent involvement activity.

- Let the students know in advance that there will be a book sharing opportunity. It makes it seem more special if the date and time are posted and an invitation is created.

- Everyone needs to do a lot of reading to consider a range of books before selecting the special one that is shared at the Book Party.

- Participants rehearse their book talks to ensure that they do not take more than two minutes and that the book talk creates interest in the listeners. They might choose a text because they have read it fully. They also could select one they are in the process of reading or are hoping to read soon.

- At the Book Party, participants sit in circles or at tables. It is very important to sit so everyone shares eye contact.

- My students really enjoy combining the book talks with refreshments to create a "party" atmosphere. You might consider serving hot chocolate with peppermint sticks for stirring, or another favorite treat.

Book Party variations:

- Cross-age gatherings of students. Think broadly here: it even works to bring Head Start children and elementary Title I students together!

- Celebrating student-authored books.

- Author studies, where each group selects an author whose books they choose.

- Theme studies, where each group selects a genre or a theme for their book selections.

- Magazine party.

- A comedy party with "Comic" moments for cartoons and comic books.

- Joke and riddle party.

- Poetry party.

Reflection Group: Self-Assessment

Name _____ Date _____

Today I participated: Too much ☐   Too little ☐   Just the right amount ☐

My most important contribution to the discussion was _____

_____

Our group is getting better at _____

_____

We still need to work on _____

_____

Rating Scale:
   5 great job
   4 pretty good
   3 I could do better
   2 I need to make a plan for improving

My score

_____	1.	I read the selection thoughtfully.
_____	2.	I marked key points in the text with sticky notes.
_____	3.	I prepared by thinking about what I would say in the group.
_____	4.	I stayed on the topic.
_____	5.	I compared the story to my life and to other books I have read.
_____	6.	I thought about critical story elements.
_____	7.	I asked questions when I didn't understand.
_____	8.	I had eye contact with members of my group.
_____	9.	I encouraged others to speak.
_____	10.	I was a good listener.

_____   My total for today

I am getting better at _____

_____

Talking About Stories

Student Name _____

Book _____

1. I read the story carefully.

2. I used the pictures to help me remember the important parts of the story.

3. I talked about the story with my partners.

4. I listened to my partners.

5. I asked questions.

6. I learned _____

_____

7. My favorite part was _____

_____

ASSESSMENT
Group Discussion Rating

Name _____ Date _____

Book _____

My Group

We knew what to do.	1 2 3 4 5	We were confused.
Everyone contributed.	1 2 3 4 5	Some people contributed.
We stayed on task.	1 2 3 4 5	We slipped off topic.
We worked together.	1 2 3 4 5	We worked independently.
We made team decisions.	1 2 3 4 5	Group decisions were difficult.

Myself

I contributed ideas.	1 2 3 4 5	I didn't say much.
I was an active listener.	1 2 3 4 5	I had a hard time listening.
I encouraged the other team members.	1 2 3 4 5	I forgot to do this.
I tried to be open to new ideas.	1 2 3 4 5	I wanted things to go my way.
I kept eye contact with the person speaking.	1 2 3 4 5	I forgot to do this.
I learned a lot today.	1 2 3 4 5	I didn't learn much today.
I am proud of my contribution today.	1 2 3 4 5	I need to try harder.

Overall rating

Great discussion.	1 2 3 4 5	We need to do better next time.

Teacher Observation: Interactions with Books

Student Name _____ Date _____

	Usually	Sometimes	Rarely
1. Engages with books independently.	☐	☐	☐
2. Chooses to read during free time.	☐	☐	☐
3. Can express thoughts about a text with an adult.	☐	☐	☐
4. Can express thoughts about a text with peers.	☐	☐	☐
5. Can justify opinions about a story.	☐	☐	☐
6. Draws on personal experiences when talking about stories.	☐	☐	☐
7. Can be specific when telling what is or is not liked about a book.	☐	☐	☐
8. Can listen to others express their thoughts.	☐	☐	☐
9. Uses references to text structure such as plot, problem, solution.	☐	☐	☐
10. Uses references to stylistic elements such as figurative language, mood, and so on.	☐	☐	☐

ASSESSMENT
Group Discussion Log

Book being discussed _____ Author _____

Date _____ Teacher _____

Key:
√   well done
–   needs support

Names of participants	#1	#2	#3	#4
Read and prepared for conversation	☐	☐	☐	☐
Noted points in text to include in discussion	☐	☐	☐	☐
Contributed to the dialogue	☐	☐	☐	☐
Asked relevant, meaningful questions	☐	☐	☐	☐
Used the text to support and clarify points	☐	☐	☐	☐
Encouraged others to talk	☐	☐	☐	☐
Made inferences beyond the text	☐	☐	☐	☐
Referred to story elements such as plot, setting, characterization, conflict, resolution	☐	☐	☐	☐
Referred to the author's use of literary elements such as mood, theme, tension, and so on	☐	☐	☐	☐

Talking About Books at Home

Dear Parent,

One of the best things you can do to assist your children with reading is to engage them in talking about the books they read. Talking stimulates language development and helps children improve their comprehension.

As you get ready to share a book with your child, you might ask your child to talk about the cover, the title, and a few of the pictures in the book. This "before-reading" conversation will help your child to build the expectation that stories make sense. This is also a good time to help your child connect personal experiences to the reading. If there is a picture showing a picnic, for example, this would be a perfect time to talk with your child about a picnic you enjoyed together.

You can also invite your child into conversation during the reading by stopping now and then to ask, "What might happen next?"

As you know, children love to share their opinions. After reading, you might get your child started with questions such as:
- What did you notice?
- What did you like?
- How did it make you feel?
- Did this remind you of any experiences you have had?
- What parts of the story were your favorites?

Just choose one or two questions so that it feels like a conversation instead of a test. Happy Reading!

Your child's teacher

2

Oral Retelling

Retelling is a reflection tool that requires readers to organize information they've gleaned from the text in order to provide a personalized summary. Students engaging in retells must review all they know about a text; select key points that reflect main ideas; consider key events, problem, solution, characters, and setting, then weave the information into a meaningful communication. Retelling has been found to significantly improve comprehension and sense of story structure (Morrow 1986) while enhancing oral language proficiency.

The following sequence provides a frame for retelling in the classroom:

- Tell the students *why* retelling is important. They need to know how a retell helps them as readers and as effective communicators. It is helpful to demonstrate storytelling by summarizing a popular movie or describing a favorite vacation to show the students how retelling fits into our lives both in and outside of school. Students can tell about family outings, about playing with their pets, or about favorite activities such as bicycling. Retelling life events is a natural part of our lives.

- Demonstrate retells that encompass key literary elements as part of Shared Book or read aloud experiences. As in all learning, "thinking aloud" about how you reviewed the text and decided what to say helps students to understand the cognitive processing they will need to implement. At this introductory stage, it is helpful to have something visual you can point to as you move through the components of the retell, such as the list on page 43 .

• Depending on the age of the students, you might want to start with a brief passage and then begin demonstrating with longer, more complex texts. It is also helpful during this demonstration stage to retell expository as well as narrative selections. While I am in this demonstration stage, I often ask the students to evaluate my retell to see if I omitted any important parts. By observing models of self-evaluation as well as the retelling process, students develop a stronger understanding of the steps they will need to follow when working independently.

Caution: It is very important to monitor authenticity of retelling experiences. If children are asked to retell a story or a life event to the same individual who listened to them read or who shared the experience, the child may perceive the interaction as a test.

• While demonstrating how to do a retell it is helpful to provide students with suggestions on how to be a good listener. Again, a visual such as the one on page 44 may help students become more effective listeners.

• Guide students as they practice. During the initial practice stage most students enjoy working in partners or groups with others who have read the same text. The activities on the following pages provide a wide range of options for this stage. It is also very helpful if students have personal samples of visuals when they are attempting their first retells.

• Another step is to work with the students to utilize voice changes, develop shifts in pacing, and add a sense of drama to the "telling" of a story. This has proven very meaningful to many students and carries over to public speaking and expressive oral reading.

• Move students closer to independence by providing retelling support in many contexts. You might want to consider having students retell:
  • the events of their weekend at home
  • at the end of independent reading when it is less likely that others are reading the same book
  • in partners so there is not a large audience
  • in the classrooms of younger students

• Help students personalize retelling as a private learning strategy. Good readers continually reflect as they read, sifting through events and understandings. Readers need to understand that retelling is something you can do privately to enhance your own understanding and memory. When internalized and applied consciously, retelling becomes a tool for lifelong learning.

To facilitate this internalization, I often stop students during independent reading time, or during a content area such as science or math, and suggest that they take a moment to reflect and do a silent retell in their head. The goal is to transfer ownership of the process to the learner.

• Student-led parent conferences are a very authentic retelling experience. When students take responsibility to tell about themselves as learners, gathering evidence of their success and offering insights about their learning, they are utilizing all key elements of a good retell.

Preparing for a Retell

1. Read a really good story.

2. List or draw the most important events from the story.

3. Read the story again to be sure that you have gotten the most important ideas.

4. Plan for any props that will make your retell interesting to an audience.

5. Practice
   - inside your head
   - to a partner
   - in front of a mirror
   - by talking into a tape recorder

6. Tell your story to an audience.

Narrative Retelling

Title and Author

Main idea: The plot

Key Characters

The Setting

The Problem

Key Events

The Resolution

Good Listeners

Have eye contact
with the storyteller

Listen carefully

Think about parts
of the retell without
talking out loud

Are ready to say
something positive
about the retell

Save questions for
the end

Storyteller's Creed

- Choose a story you like a lot.

- Read it.

- Read it again.

- Think about the story.

- Plan the performance to include information about:
  - characters
  - main character's problem
  - main events that led to solving the problem
  - the climax
  - the resolution

- Speak clearly and loudly enough for all to hear.

- Make eye contact with the audience.

- Be dramatic!

Partner Retelling

While this experience can be adapted easily to many formats, the following steps might be considered for a whole-class response to a read aloud story:

1. After reading a story to the students, explain that they will be working on retelling the story. It is helpful to identify the key points for the retelling (e.g., most important events, elements of story structure, and so on).

2. Divide the class in half so there is a storyteller group and a listening group.

3. The storytellers work in teams to reread the selection and remind each other of the focus points for this retell. The listeners also reread and reflect on what they agree to be the most important retell elements of this story.

4. The students then are matched with partners, a storyteller and a listener. While the teller talks, the listener records the elements of the story that are provided without assistance. When the storyteller is finished, it is the job of the listener to give clues about any remaining items that have not been checked off on the list.

After the students have experience with this format, it adapts easily to smaller groups of students and a wide range of texts.

Partner Retelling

Partner Retelling Activity for (story name) _____

Storyteller (name of student) _____

Listener (name of student) _____

Focus points: (Most important events, problem/solution, characters, setting)	Retold without help	Clues given
_____	☐	☐
_____	☐	☐
_____	☐	☐
_____	☐	☐
_____	☐	☐
_____	☐	☐
_____	☐	☐
_____	☐	☐
_____	☐	☐

Team Retelling

Teams of three or four students share responsibility for retelling pertinent aspects of the story structure. The retelling focus is selected by the teacher in response to needs of a group or as support for elements of text structure currently being studied. Groups might be arranged so that one team looks at problem, solution, and resolution while another team looks at literary devices such as tension, mood, and setting. It also works well to compare these structural elements across several texts.

After reflecting and talking, teams take turns retelling their stories with emphasis on the targeted elements of story design. If the teams have read different selections, the retelling becomes an authentic commercial for the focus stories, hopefully enticing listeners to engage with those same texts. If they have read the same selections, lively discussions about different interpretations can serve to deepen understanding.

I find that it is helpful to provide visuals for these activities. If each team has a set of cards identifying the elements of story structure or the literacy devices being shared during their retelling, both listeners and tellers seem to develop deeper understandings.

Variations include:

- It is sometimes fun to add an element of surprise for a group. Individual story structure cards are placed face down in front of a group and thoroughly mixed up. Group members then draw from the collection of cards to see which story element each will be responsible for telling.

- The listeners have a set of individual story structure cards. As the tellers are speaking, the listeners withdraw elements that are being described from the collection of cards. (Example: A teller explains the use of description and imagery in *Sylvester and the Magic Pebble* by William Steig and the listener removes the card for "Imagery" from the literary devices card collection.) After the telling, the listener(s) can show the teller(s) which elements they were especially aware of during the retell.

- The cards can also be used to make the organization of the retell more apparent to the listeners. The tellers might hold up the cards reflecting their focus points before beginning to tell their story and open with statements such as "Today we are going to retell the story of _____. As we tell our story, please be watching for information about [problem, solution, and theme]." This helps the listeners by giving them a focus for listening, and it helps the tellers to stay focused on their topic.

Team Retelling

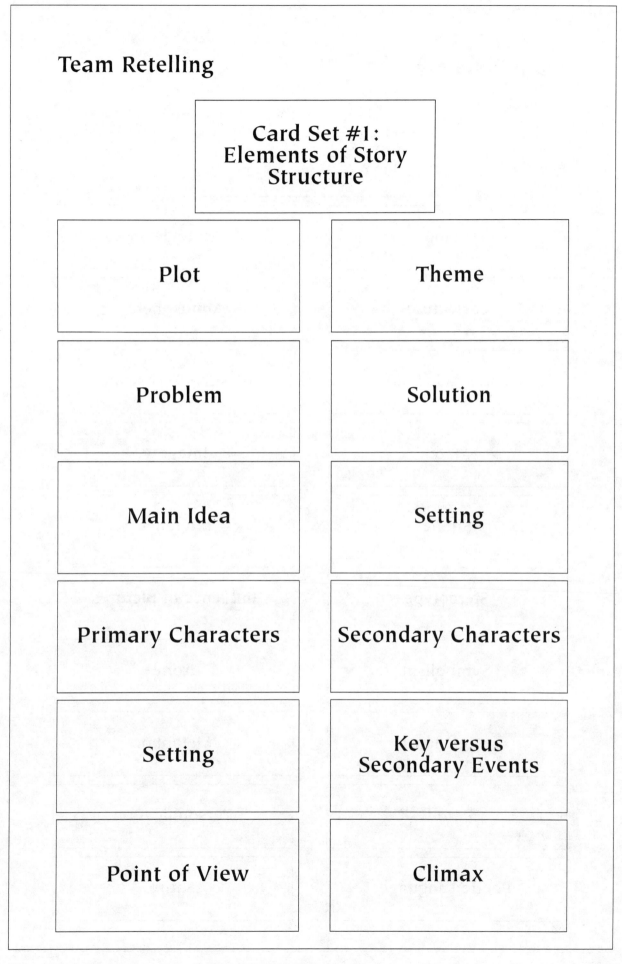

Card Set #1:
Elements of Story
Structure

Plot	Theme
Problem	Solution
Main Idea	Setting
Primary Characters	Secondary Characters
Setting	Key versus Secondary Events
Point of View	Climax

Team Retelling

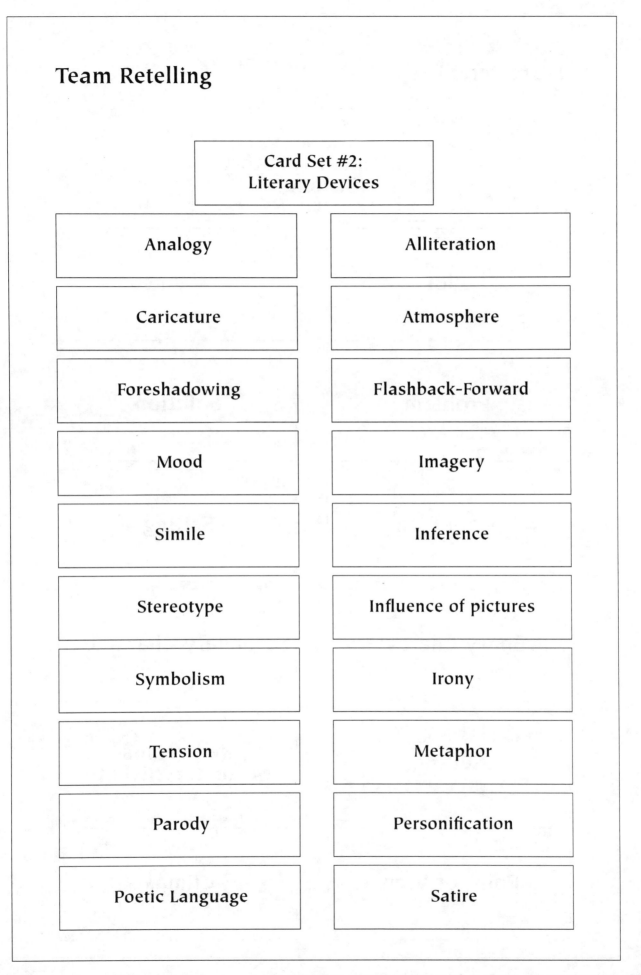

Card Set #2: Literary Devices	
Analogy	Alliteration
Caricature	Atmosphere
Foreshadowing	Flashback-Forward
Mood	Imagery
Simile	Inference
Stereotype	Influence of pictures
Symbolism	Irony
Tension	Metaphor
Parody	Personification
Poetic Language	Satire

Compare and Contrast

Name(s) of reader(s) _____ Date _____

Authors have different ways of utilizing story structure. Compare three books and consider the similarities and differences in the following areas.

	Book 1	Book 2	Book 3
Title	_____	_____	_____
	_____	_____	_____
The setting	_____	_____	_____
	_____	_____	_____
	_____	_____	_____
The problem	_____	_____	_____
	_____	_____	_____
	_____	_____	_____
The climax	_____	_____	_____
	_____	_____	_____
	_____	_____	_____
The ending	_____	_____	_____
	_____	_____	_____
	_____	_____	_____

Newscast

For this retelling activity, I make a videotape of a local news broadcast and then invite the students to analyze it. Students discuss the pacing, the way newscasters look right at the camera, the strategy of telling main ideas, the use of video clips of the action, and so forth.

Students work in teams of two to develop "newscasts" to retell favorite stories or recount key points from a unit of study.

Props can make this seem more official. I find that younger students enjoy standing behind a cardboard cutout of a television set with a "microphone." Older students enjoy sitting behind a table at the front of the class much like they see in a television newscast or talk show.

To support students in preparing for their newscasts, it is helpful to teach them a recounting format that is based on journalism techniques.

Recounts include:

Who	What	When
Where	How	Why

Interview ideas:

- Interview the principal or another staff member about a school event. Conduct the interview in front of an audience or videotape it to show at a later time.

- Have a student take the role of a character from a book. Then interview the "character" as above.

Game Show

Students meet in teams to develop retells of familiar stories. The tellers include references to characters, events, and the problem/solution, but do not tell the name of the story or use the specific names of characters. The listeners in the audience must guess the name of the story.

Game Show Planning Sheet

Teller(s) _____ Date _____

The Story _____

Plan to include:
    Characters
    Events
    Problem
    Solution
    Climax

How will you avoid using the names of the characters or mentioning the name of the story?

Which clues are least or most likely to help your listeners guess the name of the story? (You might want to save those for the end of your retell.)

Paper Bag Theater

Students illustrate a key setting from a story on the front of a paper lunch bag. They then illustrate and cut out drawings that represent characters and elements of the setting that the readers believe will make the story more interesting to a listener.

When the visuals are completed, the teller stands behind the Paper Bag Theater and begins telling the story while pulling out the appropriate visuals to support the story line.

Story Bag

Students collect realia representing key points in the story and place them in a bag. They then use these real items as storytelling props. For example, a Story Bag for Cinderella might have a cleaning rag, a high-heeled shoe, a pumpkin, and a clock.

Storytelling at the Overhead

Students use overhead transparencies to draw the characters and setting elements from a favorite story. They then stand at the overhead to do their retelling, using the visuals they have created.

Wearable Art

Younger students really enjoy wearing storytelling aprons, storytelling vests, and storytelling hats. The apron and vest can be made from felt with minimal amounts of sewing. The storytelling hat can be made by taking any suitable hat and covering the dome with sticky-back Velcro strips.

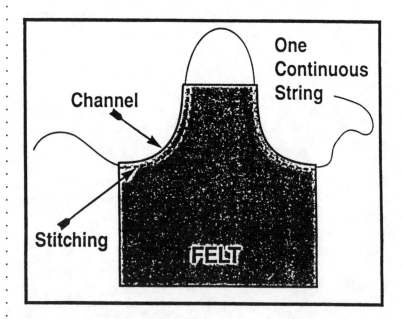

FIGURE 2–1 Apron pattern

The Process   Students draw the characters and props that they want to use in retelling a story on heavyweight tag paper. Then, they apply sticky-backed Velcro to the back of their illustrations. The illustrations should be large enough to be seen from several feet away. When they go to perform their retell, the students can wear their felt vest, apron, or hat and adhere their Velcro-backed art to the garment as they tell the story.

Spin a Story

Team members take turns spinning an arrow that is attached to a tag-board playing surface. Each time their spinner lands on a category, players need to tell something relevant to that dimension of the story. For example, if a student spins and lands on Events, the student would tell about one event. The board is then passed to the next player. That player spins and lands on Characters and then tells something about a character or character development, and so on.

The categories on the playing surface should reflect current teaching points for story structure or areas in which these particular students need additional support.

Spinner #1

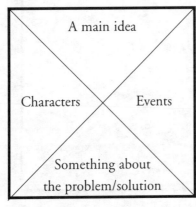

Spinner #2

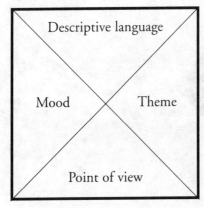

Spin a Story

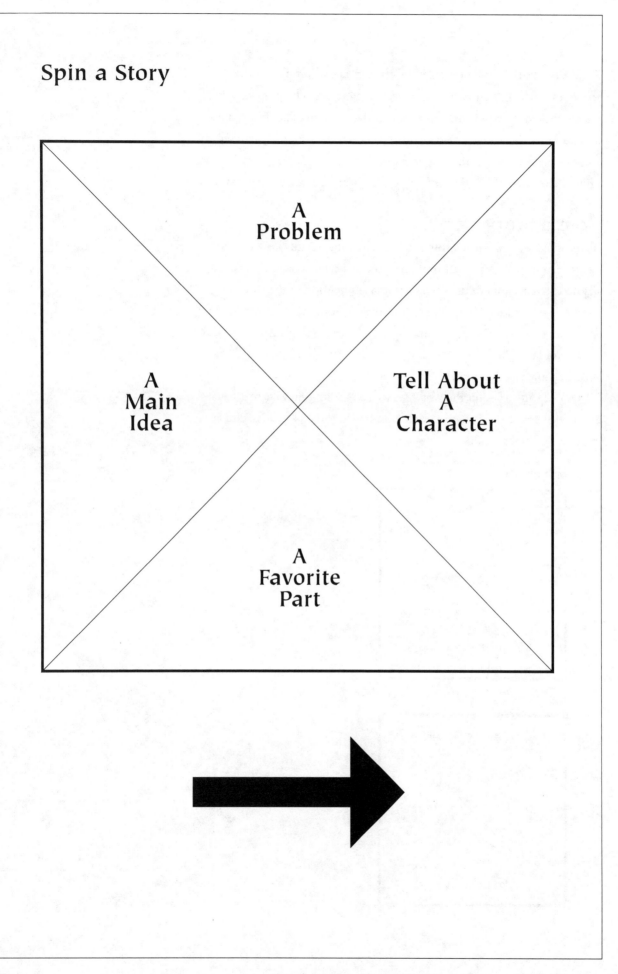

A Trick of the Hand

Have students trace around their hands, making sure to go between each finger. Then on each finger of the tracing, students can write an element of story structure they want to remember in their retelling (e.g., the main idea).

Storytelling Glove

Using newly purchased white garden gloves, write storytelling elements on each finger of the glove and place a heart in the center for the author's message. Students can then wear the glove while rehearsing for retelling.

Food handler's gloves can also be used for this purpose and are a very inexpensive way to provide parents with take-home versions of the Storytelling Glove.

FIGURE 2–2 Elements of a story
Thanks to Debbie Bodine.

Book Reviews on Tape

Book Reviews can take many forms. One of my favorites is to invite students to make an audiotape of a retell for a favorite book, place it in a zip-lock bag that attaches to the inside cover of the book. Students who are book browsing and making selections of books to read can elect to listen to the retell as part of their process of deciding whether or not to read this book.

Spicing It Up with Line Drawings

Students who enjoy drawing often enjoy illustrating *while* they tell a story. They can stand in front of an easel with a felt pen and create line drawings as they talk about story elements. It also works well to have students stand at the chalkboard or at the overhead to draw as they retell.

Expert Panels on Books

Students read the text several times and prepare to deal with audience questions such as How was suspense maintained? What was critical in the interaction between characters? How does the plot reflect real life? In the meantime, the audience prepares a list of questions to ask the "expert."

Cumulative Retells

This activity involves physical movement and lots of repetition. Like cumulative story structure, it is an add-on format where everything that is already known is repeated each time a new element of the retell is added.

After reading a story, I ask a volunteer to come to the front of the room and "tell" the first event from the story. A second volunteer comes forward to tell the second event but before that person tells it, the first student repeats event #1. A cumulative retell for Cinderella might sound something like:

Step 1. Teller #1: Once upon a time there was a girl named Cinderella who lived with her stepmother and stepsisters.

Step 2. Teller #1: Once upon a time there was a girl named Cinderella who lived with her stepmother and stepsisters.

Teller #2: She had to clean and work and was called Cinderella because she had to clean the ashes out of the fireplace.

Step 3. Teller #1: Once upon a time there was a girl named Cinderella who lived with her stepmother and stepsisters.

Teller #2: She had to clean and work and was called Cinderella because she had to clean the ashes out of the fireplace.

Teller #3: The stepsisters were very excited because they were buying beautiful dresses to wear to a ball at the palace,

and so on.

The students love the repetition and the rhythm that develops as this process unfolds, and I find that challenged learners are especially supported by the fun-filled repetition of story elements. A variation to this would be to have audience members make up a physical action for each teller's event so they are physically involved even as listeners.

Story Journey

This is a structure to support students who indicate they need greater support in understanding shifts in setting.

1. After reading, I have students review a selection and place a sticky note at the top of pages that represent a *change* in setting.

2. Once they know how many settings were in the story, they can quickly sketch backgrounds (like the backdrop in a play) for each setting. It is important for the students to understand that characters cannot be placed in the background. Characters will be considered separately.

3. Puppets are created for each character in the story and placed on a stick.

4. Readers are now ready to talk about each setting and decide which characters were present in that setting.

5. Finally, the students present the retell by describing each setting and the actions of the characters who were present.

Form for Story Journey

The Book _____   The Teller(s) _____

An illustration is created for each setting and characters move along a path between each one. This process is especially powerful when done on large sheets of butcher paper so the students can physically move when they change settings.

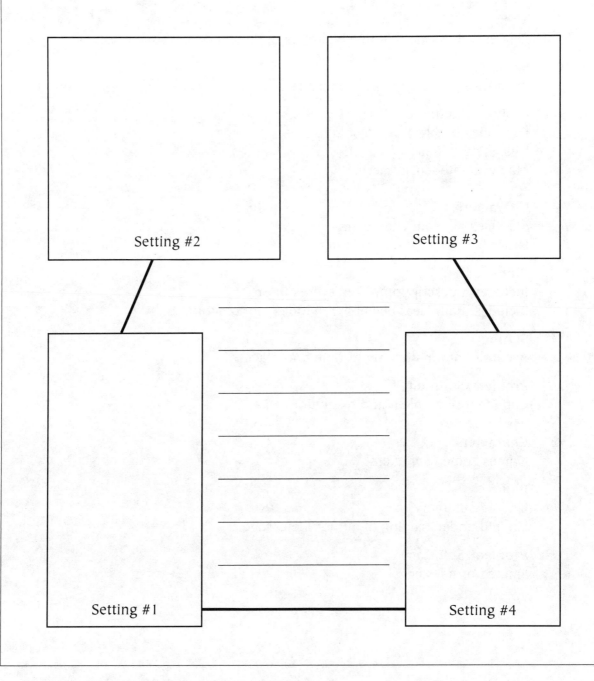

Setting #2

Setting #3

Setting #1

Setting #4

Scoring Guide: Reading Retell

6 Characters
Describes all main and secondary characters
Describes traits of main characters

Plot
Provides analysis, including inferences
Makes personal connections to the story
Retells main and secondary events in order with detail

Theme
Relates a message that demonstrates understanding of world issues

Setting
Includes specific details about place or time

Problem/Solution
Describes problem and resolution
Designates climax
May evaluate tension level

4 Characters
Identifies all main characters
Describes some character traits

Plot
Includes a description of key events in order
Includes main idea, beginning, middle, end of story

Setting
Accurate information about time and place

Problem/Solution
Can identify problem and resolution

2 Characters
Names some characters

Plot
Limited summary
Limited understanding of author's message

Problem/Solution
Limited or missing

Partner Retelling Checklist

Name of Partner _____   Name of Listener _____

Date _____   Book _____

Draw a circle around one thing your partner did *very* well today. Put a
check next to one suggestion for improvement and tell your partner WHY.

The main idea

The characters

The setting

The most important events

The problem

The solution

ASSESSMENT
Teacher Checklist: Story Retelling

Student's Name _____ Date _____ Age/Grade _____

Title and Author of Book _____

		Minimum	Moderate	Excellent
1.	Accurately retells literal information	☐	☐	☐
2.	Includes inferred information	☐	☐	☐
3.	Provides information about characters	☐	☐	☐
4.	Describes the setting	☐	☐	☐
5.	Includes a summary or a generalization	☐	☐	☐
6.	Restates the problem and solution	☐	☐	☐
7.	Makes evaluative statements or generates a question about the text	☐	☐	☐
8.	Relates personal knowledge or experience to the text	☐	☐	☐

Personal Reflection: Retelling Checklist

Name _____ Date _____

Story _____

Opening:
☐ I began my retelling with an introduction.

Setting
☐ I included when and where the story happened.

Characters
☐ I told about the main character.
☐ I told about other characters.

Problem
☐ I told about the problem of the story.

Solution
☐ I told how the problem was solved.
☐ I told how the story ended.

Author's Message
☐ I shared my ideas about the author's message.

The best part of my retelling was _____

_____

The next time I retell, I need to remember _____

_____

My audience was _____

_____

Retelling: Self-Evaluation

Name _____

When I think about my retells, I know
I am good at: _____

_____

_____

_____

I am working on: _____

_____

_____

_____

My goal as a storyteller is: _____

_____

_____

_____

ASSESSMENT
Retelling Profile: Plot Structure

Teller _____ Date _____

Text _____ Listener _____

	Minimal Information				Very Complete
Characters	1	2	3	4	5
Setting	1	2	3	4	5
Plot	1	2	3	4	5
Problem	1	2	3	4	5
Solution	1	2	3	4	5
Personal Inferences	1	2	3	4	5

Retelling Profile: Literary Elements

Teller _____   Date _____

Text _____ Listener _____

	Minimal Information				Very Complete
Theme	1	2	3	4	5
Plot	1	2	3	4	5
Mood	1	2	3	4	5
Tension	1	2	3	4	5
Structure	1	2	3	4	5

Unassisted Retell Observation

Teller _____ Age _____

Instructor _____ Listener _____

	Date _____	Date _____	Date _____
	Book _____	Book _____	Book _____
	_____	_____	_____
	Score (1-5)	Score (1-5)	Score (1-5)
Setting	_____	_____	_____
Complete Event Sequence	_____	_____	_____
Problem	_____	_____	_____
Solution	_____	_____	_____
Overall Retell	_____	_____	_____

Comments: _____

Book 1 _____

_____

Book 2 _____

_____

Book 3 _____

_____

Classroom Retelling Profile

Key:
+   Information given without prompts
√   Information given with prompts
0   Information not given

Student name	Book	Characters	Plot: Events	Theme	Setting	Prob/Solution

Data can be collected over multiple retellings. Patterns of performance can be easily detected in a particular dimension of the retell, such as character, plot, and so on.

Parent Page: The Story Star

Retelling stories helps children understand books better. Please take a few minutes to invite your child to retell a story that you have shared together. As your child talks, you might want to be looking at the Story Star on page 72 to give your child clues about story components that may have been omitted. As your child gains confidence, you might ask your child to use the Story Star to plan a retell for you and/or the family, then "perform" when he or she is ready.

The Story Star

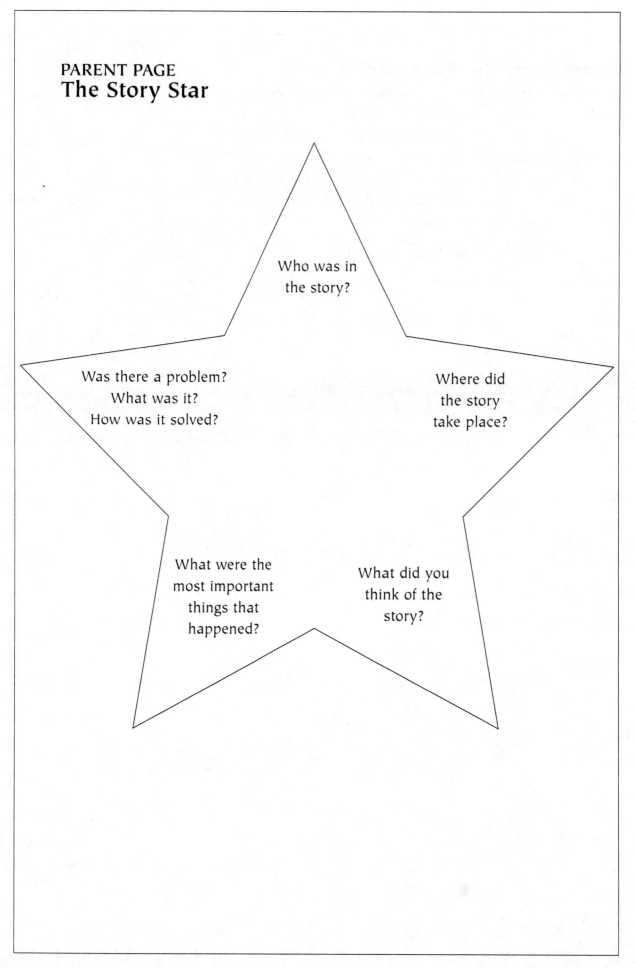

Who was in
the story?

Was there a problem?
What was it?
How was it solved?

Where did
the story
take place?

What were the
most important
things that
happened?

What did you
think of the
story?

PARENT PAGE
Observation Guide

Name of Child _____

This reflection completed by _____ Date _____

When listening to a story, my child:	Usually	Sometimes	Rarely
Looks closely at the pictures	☐	☐	☐
Looks at or points to words	☐	☐	☐
Responds to the meaning by making comments, laughing, etc.	☐	☐	☐
Gives an opinion about the story	☐	☐	☐

When retelling a story, my child:			
Speaks clearly and can be understood	☐	☐	☐
Uses eye contact with listeners	☐	☐	☐
Includes main events from the story	☐	☐	☐
Includes key characters	☐	☐	☐
Mentions the setting for the story	☐	☐	☐
Can tell about the problem in the story and how it was solved	☐	☐	☐

3

· ·

Written Reflections

When children write, they read. When children write, they think and reflect. When children write, they utilize all they know about sounds, symbols, the structures of language, and the construction of meaning (Calkins 1986). In an ideal language-learning classroom, children should be writing all day long. They should write to fulfill a basic human need for expression. They should write for the joy of it. They should write to remember. They should write in authentic, meaningful ways and then write some more.

Writing has been long understood as a tool for development of long-term memory and for deepening understanding. When the power of writing is combined with the power of retelling, students are immersed in a language-learning atmosphere that is charged with possibility. Writing develops both thinking and learning by creating a means for learners to modify and extend their understanding.

The structures that follow are designed to be *one small part* of a broad and richly developed classroom writing program.

Written Retells

Written retells are easy to prepare and naturally accommodate all developmental levels; they are perfect vehicles for increasing learner responsibility while deepening understanding of published and student-authored texts (Brown and Cambourne 1987). They assist learners in fine-tuning their understanding of text structure, while enhancing their achievements as readers and writers. In their dual role as instructional and assessment tools, retells can be analyzed for a wide range of understandings about both the published text and the writer's understanding of written language.

Story Map

This is about: ☐ a book   ☐ a real event

Writer _____   Date _____

1. Draw a picture of one main idea in each of the boxes below.
2. Cut out the boxes and glue them on a large sheet of paper.
3. Draw arrows between the boxes to show the order.
4. Write about each picture.
5. Tell someone about your work. Be sure to tell why you chose the parts
    you selected.

Retelling from the Heart

Sometimes writers forget that small moments in life can make wonderful stories. The following visualization experience is designed to assist writers in finding the stories within their own lives that are well worth telling.

Narrowing the Focus

1. Ask students to write down three special memories or things they really enjoy doing.

2. After providing time for quiet reflection, ask each student to tell someone close to them about the three things on their list.

3. Have students mark the one that seemed easiest to talk about.

Visualizing

1. Guide students through a visualization experience using all of their senses. As you guide their internal reflections, stop often and ask them to write words and phrases or draw pictures that reflect the images rolling through their thoughts. You might make statements such as "As you imagine yourself in the middle of this special time, what do you see around you? Please write words and phrases that describe what you see."

2. Continue the visualization and list-making process as you direct their thinking to sounds, smells, things to touch, and feelings related to this special something in their lives.

Writing

1. Invite students to begin writing about this special memory or pleasant experience. They might want to use words and phrases from the list they made or to draw images from a picture they drew while going through the visualization.

2. Provide opportunities to share their writing and to talk about the experience.

3. I have students tuck writing experiences such as this into their writing folders or into their writers notebooks.

The goal of this experience is not necessarily a finished piece of writing, but rather a better understanding of how to reach inside and pull out writing that is rich with descriptors and feelings—a retell in the most personal sense.

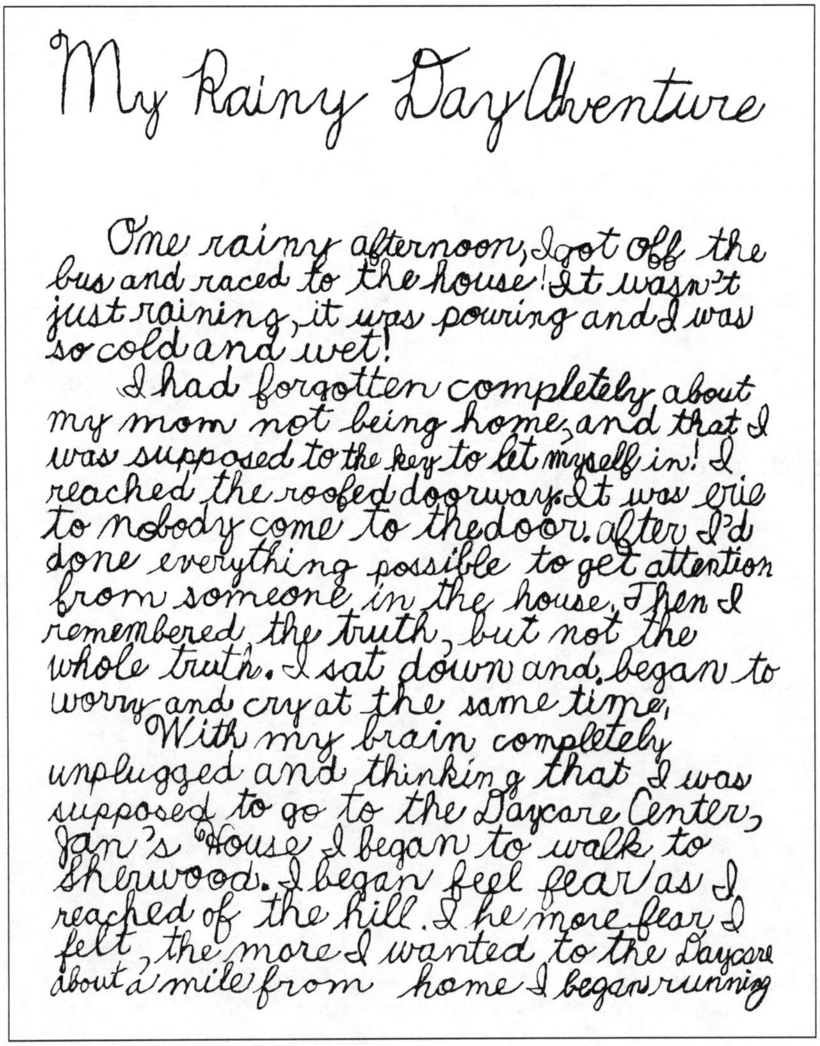

My Rainy Day Adventure

One rainy afternoon, I got off the bus and raced to the house! It wasn't just raining, it was pouring and I was so cold and wet!

I had forgotten completely about my mom not being home, and that I was supposed to the key to let myself in! I reached the roofed doorway. It was erie to nobody come to the door. After I'd done everything possible to get attention from someone in the house, Then I remembered the truth, but not the whole truth. I sat down and began to worry and cry at the same time.

With my brain completely unplugged and thinking that I was supposed to go to the Daycare Center, Jan's House I began to walk to Sherwood. I began feel fear as I reached of the hill. The more fear I felt, the more I wanted to the Daycare about a mile from home I began running

FIGURE 3–1 My Rainy Day Adventure

Book Rating

Student _____ Date _____

The Book _____ Author _____

This book was:

☐ So good I couldn't put it down
☐ Pretty interesting
☐ OK
☐ Not great

Tell why you rated the book this way. Please be specific.

If you were to pass this book along to a friend, what would you say?

Book Review: Narrative

Name: _____ Date: _____

Title of Book _____ Author _____

Illustrator _____

My opinion of the story:

My opinion of the illustrations:

My recommendations to others about this book:

Story Reflections

Draw a picture about the story.

_____
One word about the main character

_____ , _____
Two words describing the setting

_____ , _____ , _____
Three words telling the problem

_____ , _____ , _____ , _____
Four words about an event

_____ , _____ , _____ , _____ , _____
Five words about the solution

Story Scaffold

Name of Student _____

Title of Story _____

This story begins when _____

_____

The problem is _____

_____

The next thing that happens is _____

_____

Then _____

_____

After that, _____

_____

The problem is solved when _____

_____

Image Search: The Art of Good Writing

Name _____ Date _____

Please select three books that you are familiar with and either reread them or skim through them, searching for points where the author has used descriptive language to build strong visual images. Please use sticky notes to mark your favorite points in each book, then choose the *very best* example from each book. After you make your selections, think about how you will share them with others. You may want to practice reading them aloud with expression or think of how you can help others develop an appreciation for the rich language in your samples.

Example #1: From (book) _____

This excerpt came from page: _____

Written by _____

Example #2: From (book) _____

This excerpt came from page: _____

Written by _____

Example #3: From (book) _____

This excerpt came from page: _____

Written by _____

What did you learn about descriptive writing?

How will you change your own writing as a result of what you learned?

My Character Says

Knowing that comprehension deepens significantly when a reader can experience understanding from multiple perspectives, My Character Says is designed as a strategy to help learners examine a character or historical figure in greater depth. Students work in teams of two, each choosing to "become" a different character from a story or historical event. They share one piece of paper.

One student opens by writing a question for the other to answer. There should be *no talking!*

Example #1	Example #2
Responding to *Little Red Riding Hood*	Responding to *The Sign of the Beaver*
Hi, Mr. Wolf. What are you doing? *I am going into the forest.* Oh, that's nice. *Where are you going?* To my Grandma's house. *OK. Bye.* Goodbye! *Wait. What do you have in* *the basket?* Some treats for my Grandma.	Hey Matt. Why do you look at books and paper when you could be out hunting? *I like to read. I learn about places* *I have never visited and I learn* *how to do things.* *Would you like me to teach you* *to read, Attean?* Yes. I would like to learn white man's book words.

Interactive Journals

For Emergent Writers

Materials   a large sheet of paper folded in half for every student

Step #1. Each student draws and writes about a story or learning experience using one half of the paper.

Step #2. Partners talk about their drawing, their writing, and their reflections.

Step #3. The partners trade papers.

Step #4. Using the second section on their partner's paper, each student draws and writes a response to their partner's work. This might take the form of adding information, voicing a shared thought about the story, or something else.

Step #5. Sharing. Partners meet in larger groups to talk about their shared drawing and writing.

Partner 1   Partner 2

FIGURE 3–2 Response to *The Very Hungry Caterpillar*

For More Fluent Writers

Materials   8.5-x-11-inch paper, folded into fourths, then opened flat. Number the quadrants 1 through 4. This works best immediately following a learning opportunity such as reading, discussing, problem solving.

Step #1. Students gather in teams of three. Each team member has his or her own paper and pencil or pen. They need to know that there will be an audience for their writing as other members of their group will read and respond to what they write.

Step #2. All students begin writing and reflecting in quadrant #1. Their writing might be stimulated with questions such as "What did you think about the story?" "What personal connections were there for you?" "What is the most important thought to remember about the Civil War?" and so on.

Step #3. At a predetermined signal, have the students pass their papers within their group of three. (I usually have everyone pass to the right to avoid confusion.) They now are holding someone else's paper. The task is to read what is written in quadrant #1 and then respond in quadrant #2 with additional thoughts, reactions, or shared feelings.

Step #4. The students pass their papers one more time. This time they read quadrant #1 and quadrant #2, then respond in #3.

Step #5. All papers return to their original owners. The owner of the paper reads all responses and then reflects in quadrant #4. This self-reflection might include thoughts such as "Do I still feel the same as I did in quadrant #1?" "Did I learn anything new?" "What lingering questions do I have?"

#1 Evan	#2 Marcus
I don't think the drinking age should be lowered to 18. The papers are full of stories about teenagers in car accidents because they have been drinking. It doesn't make sense to make the problem worse.	I see your point about driving but it also doesn't make sense to me that an 18-year-old can go in in the army and be old enough to vote but can't drink legally.
#3 Juan	#4 Evan
I think that the driving age should be changed too. Maybe there are so many teenage accidents because teenagers just aren't ready to drive. My brother drives but he isn't responsible enough to do his homework.	I wonder if there should be one age for everything. Voting, driving, and legal drinking should happen when you can act and think like an adult. I wonder what age would be best.

Creating a Story Chain

Using strips of paper that are two inches wide and six inches long, have students create a story chain. Each link of the chain could represent:

- A key event from a picture book
- Literary elements such as tension, mood, or imagery
- Characters, problem, solution, and so on

With chapter books, students can focus on setting, problem, solution, characters, key event, and prediction for each chapter. It is helpful to change colors with each chapter or area of focus.

It's in the Can!

For a novel format, students sometimes enjoy writing their retells on adding machine tape. They then roll up the paper tape and place it inside a coffee can. The paper tape can be slowly pulled out through a slit cut into the plastic lid of the can and read by individuals who may be interested in that particular book.

Instant Book Reviews

Invite readers and writers to use a sticky note and write a VERY SHORT review about a book they read and then stick it inside the front cover of the book. As other students browse looking for books to read, they can read these instant reviews and consider them as they decide whether or not to engage with that particular book. Some students also enjoy adding a numerical rating. For example: On a scale of 1-10, this book is a _____.

Pass Around Retells

Students meet in teams of three or four. Each person has their own sheet of paper. At a signal, everyone begins writing a retell of the story on their own paper. When a timer rings, the papers are passed to the right. Each writer now has someone else's paper. The task is to read what has been written so far and continue the story from that point. When the timer rings again, the papers pass once more and the writing goes on. I find that students really appreciate the various points of view and do some in-depth thinking about which elements of a retell are really critical.

Create and Assess a Graphic Organizer

Guide students who have had extensive experience with written retells and graphic organizers to create an organizer to match a story. This places far more responsibility on the learner than a teacher-generated organizer and often results in very creative responses to the text.

Ideally, students would generate their own scoring guide with attributes of well-crafted organizers. The one that follows gives them some ideas:

5 The problem, main events, and conclusion are well described
Important characters are all mentioned
The setting is described in detail
Events are included in correct sequence
The problem and solution are clearly stated and explained

3 The story map is adequate
Problem, main events, and conclusion are included with some description
Most characters are mentioned
The setting is mentioned but not described
The events are mostly in sequence
The problem and solution are mentioned but not explained

1 Little effort
Unsatisfactory attempt

My Favorites

Name _____ Date _____

Of all the books I have read, _____ has the best beginning.

The author is _____

I liked the beginning because _____

_____

_____

Of all the books I have read, _____ has the best middle.

The author is _____

I liked the middle because _____

_____

_____

Of all the books I have read, _____ has the best ending.

The author is _____

I liked the ending because _____

_____

_____

Key Word Strategy

1. Read a story.
2. Reread it with the goal of trying to select a few key words that seem especially important to the story. Make a list of these words. Be selective. You want the MOST IMPORTANT words.
3. Cut your list apart so that each word can be moved separately.
4. Arrange the words in a way that supports you as you retell the story in your head. (For example, in Cinderella "fireplace" and "cinders" would probably come before "pumpkin.")
5. Use your words to get you started writing a summary of the story.

The Reader _____ Date _____

The Book _____

Key Word List

My summary:

How many of your key words appeared in your summary?

Terquain

Reader _____

Draw a picture about a book, a special character, or something you are learning about. Follow the steps below to create a three-line poem

```



```

The Topic _____

_____

Two or Three Words About the Topic _____

_____

A Feeling or Synonym Related to the Topic _____

_____

Creating a Readers Theater Script

Readers theater scripts are powerful tools for helping students to read and write reflectively. To create a script, writers must read carefully, weighing critical points against those less worthy of attention. They then need to craft language that sounds fluent when read aloud. They also need to stretch into inferential reasoning to determine how voices should sound and how a narrator might assist the mood through carefully chosen comments.

Scripts for Expository Learning

The following example came from a fourth-grade student. He was asked to write a report about Abraham Lincoln, and he promptly began groaning and exhibiting every avoidance behavior he had in his bag of tricks. When the assignment was reconfigured to "Write a readers theater script that you can perform with two friends," he was suddenly filled with enthusiasm and eagerly began researching and writing. What a change!

Example *Abraham Lincoln* by Brenden

NARRATOR #1: In 1890 Abraham Lincoln was born in a log cabin in Kentucky. He moved a lot as a child.

NARRATOR #2: When he was nine, his mother, and her aunt, and her uncle died leaving his father to take care of Abe, his sister, and his second cousin.

NARRATOR #1: A year later, Abe's father left on a trip and the kids were left at home for many weeks.

EVERYONE: When his father returned, he had a new wife.

NARRATOR #2: Abraham worked hard to learn to read and write. He was also a hard laborer. He cut wood and even worked on the Mississippi River.

Scripts for Novels and Picture Books

To create readers theater scripts with novels or picture books, students review the text to determine which events were most critical to the story line. They then review the narration and dialogue for each event and select the critical portions. It helps to work with photocopies of the text when they are at this stage so they can cross out and highlight as they discuss. Finally, they write their summaries of the dialogue and narration into a script.

Example *Cinderella* by Megan

STEPMOTHER: Cinderella! Get in here right now. The prince is about to arrive with the glass slipper for your sisters to try on and this place is a mess!

CINDERELLA: Yes. Of course I will help you.

NARRATOR #1: She said in a sweet and patient voice.

NARRATOR #2: As Cinderella entered the room, her hand closed around the glass slipper that was tucked safely into her apron pocket.

STEPMOTHER: While you are cleaning, be sure to start a fire and then hurry quickly to start a pot of tea. It is very important that you get done and get back to the kitchen with the cook. We wouldn't want you in the way when the prince arrives.

NARRATOR #1: She said with a sneer.

Create a Readers Theater Script

Narrator #1: _____

_____

_____

_____

Narrator #2: _____

_____

_____

_____

Narrator #3: _____

_____

_____

_____

Everyone: _____

_____

_____

_____

The Important Thing About . . .

This structure helps students focus on main ideas and works equally well with a wide range of textual understandings. Students can use this to consider an entire story, a key character, a literacy device used in the story, a person in their lives, or other themes.

Adapted from *The Important Book,* by Margaret Wise Brown.

The Important Thing About . . .

Writer _____ Date _____

Topic _____

The important thing about _____

is that _____

_____

_____

It is true that _____

_____

_____

But, the important thing about _____

is that _____

_____

_____

Riddling Along

Students love riddles and jokes and often enjoy creating riddles about characters, key events, or information gained from a unit of study.

Focus on a character

She was pretty.

She worked hard.

She had two stepsisters who were mean to her.

She had a fairy godmother.

She went to a ball and lost her glass slipper.

When it turned midnight, she ran home in rags.

Who is it?

Answer: _____

Focus on a unit of study

This animal has a large pouch under its beak.

It can scoop up a fish and carry it inside the pouch.

Answer: _____

Riddling Along

Topic for my riddle _____

Name of author _____ Date _____

1. List facts you know on this topic:

2. Number your facts. Number 1 should be the fact least likely to give away the answer to your riddle. The highest number should go to the fact that would most likely give away the answer.

3. Rewrite the facts in the order you chose (Numbers 1 to —) and think of an ending question.

4. Read your riddle to others and see if they can guess the answer.

Writing Letters

Students who write letters to show what they know have an opportunity to explore their own meanings, express themselves through written language, and engage in social dialogue, all while practicing a genre that is useful throughout life.

Here is an example from health class:

Dear Jenny,

Did you know that babies have 300 bones in their bodies? I have been reading about the human body, and I learned that bones grow together so that when you are older you only have 206 bones.

I also learned that the center of our bones makes our red blood cells. Red blood cells carry oxygen and give us energy.

Megan

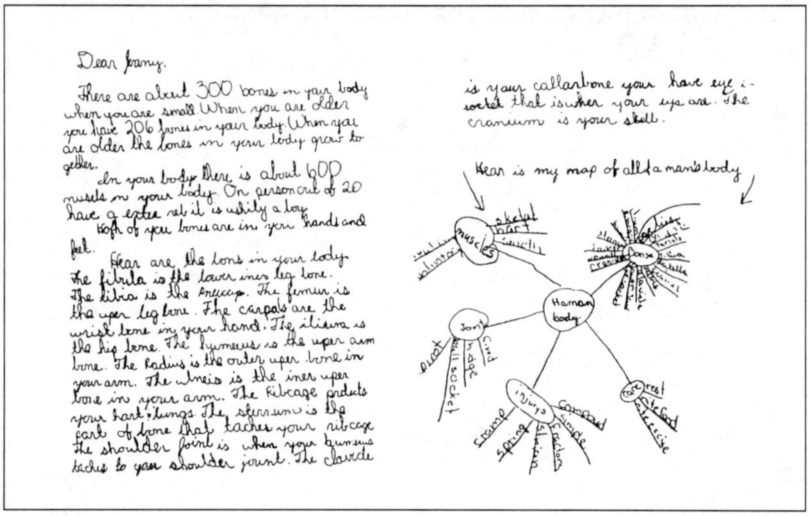

FIGURE 3–3 Writing letters

Here is an example from math class:

Dear Mom,

We are learning about fractions. At first I thought they were hard but then the teacher brought in apples and candy bars. We cut them into parts and had to tell how much we were eating. I got to eat 1/6 of an apple and 1/4 of a candy bar. I guess fractions aren't so hard.

Love,

Kyle

Thumbnail Sketch

1. Ask students to review a text and then use five sentences or less to summarize the *most important* thoughts.

2. Writers then get together with a partner or a team to come to consensus about a group "thumbnail" sketch that uses five sentences or less and covers points that everyone agrees are most important.

Thumbnail Sketch: Group Format

Writer(s) _____   Date _____

My personal thumbnail sketch was about . . .

Our group had some really good ideas about . . .

The group summary included the following ideas that were also in my summary . . .

The group summary included the following ideas that were additions to the summary I wrote . . .

Literature News

A Newspaper Template for Headlines and Stories About Books

Headline example   Cleaning Girl Marries Prince

Article example:

Cinderella, a former cleaning girl who worked for her stepmother and stepsisters, has announced her marriage to the prince. The prince spotted the beautifully dressed girl at his formal ball, fell in love, and made her his princess. Cinderella claims to have a fairy godmother who made the match possible.

Writing Newsletters About Real School Events

Example:

On December third, three- and four-year-olds came to school. They came from the Head Start Program. The fourth and fifth graders from our school had practiced reading books to read to the preschoolers. Each preschooler got to be with students from our school to listen to a story and have cookies and punch.

Borders Book Reviews

Borders Books, like many other bookstores, produces a newsletter profiling activities and new books on the market. In Beaverton, Oregon, Borders invites students from local schools to write reviews and then the student-authored reviews are published in the newsletter!

FIGURE 3–4   Borders Book Review

Just Like

Readers select a character from a book and list traits of that character in the first column. For each trait, readers need to read across the columns to decide if they also have that trait (column 2), if someone they know has that trait (column 3), or if another character has that trait.

Example   Cinderella

Column 1	Column 2	Column 3	Column 4
List Traits	Like Myself?	Like a Friend?	Like Another Character?
Hardworking	√	Alicia	Little Red Hen
Patient	–	My teacher	The Little Engine That Could

Just Like

Name _____ Date _____

Book _____

The Character: _____

Character Traits	Like Myself?	Like a Friend?	Like Another Character?

Action!

Name of Reader/Writer _____ Date _____

Book _____ Focus Character _____

The Problem Is _____

Influence on Problem

↑

Result

↑

Action

Dual Bio Poems

My name _____ The character _____

Book _____ Date _____

	Myself	Character
Name	_____	_____
Four Adjectives	_____	_____
	_____	_____
	_____	_____
	_____	_____
Who feels	_____	_____
Who needs	_____	_____
Who likes	_____	_____
Who would like to	_____	_____
Name	_____	_____

Point It Out!

The Reader/Writer _____

The Book _____

Identify key words and phrases that, in very few words, bring about strong visual images.

Key Words and Phrases

Produces strong images about:
(List character, setting, event, problem, emotion)

1._____   _____

2._____   _____

3._____   _____

4._____   _____

5._____   _____

6._____   _____

7._____   _____

8._____   _____

Share your choices and tell *why* you selected them.

Response Points:
- What did I learn about the craft of writing?
- How can I use this in my writing today and in the future?

Focus on Emotions

The Reader/Writer _____

The Book _____

Significant Emotions in This Book	My Reflections/Observations
	How were these emotions made clear? What did the author do to develop the reader's understanding? Show examples of the author's craft.

1. _____   _____

_____

_____

2. _____   _____

_____

_____

3. _____   _____

_____

_____

Response Points
- What did I learn about the craft of writing?
- How can I use this in my writing today and in the future?

Character Analysis

Character Analysis for (name of character) _____

Name of Book _____ Reader/Writer _____

	Strength	Weakness	Why?
Listening	☐	☐	_____
			_____
Facing challenges	☐	☐	_____
			_____
Solving problems	☐	☐	_____
			_____
Being creative	☐	☐	_____
			_____
Demonstrating patience	☐	☐	_____
			_____
Getting along with others	☐	☐	_____
			_____

Other traits: _____

_____

_____

Attribute Graph

Work with the students to select a focus for this interaction. The focus might be attributes of a character, an author, a historical figure, the climax of a story, and so on.

Students discuss the attributes graph and list the attributes they agree to be most significant and/or well developed at the bottom of the graph. They then evaluate each attribute on a scale of 1 to 10.

Attribute Graph for *Cinderella*

	Kind	Thoughtful	Creative	Generous	Wicked	Mean	Hardworking		
10	▓	▓					▓		
9	▓	▓					▓		
8	▓	▓					▓		
7	▓	▓					▓		
6	▓	▓					▓		
5	▓	▓		▓			▓		
4	▓	▓		▓			▓		
3	▓	▓		▓			▓		
2	▓	▓		▓			▓		
1	▓	▓		▓			▓		
Attributes	Kind	Thoughtful	Creative	Generous	Wicked	Mean	Hardworking		

Attribute Graph

Name _____

Attribute Analysis for _____

10									
9									
8									
7									
6									
5									
4									
3									
2									
1									
Attributes									

If I Were the Author

Name _____   Date _____

Book Title _____   Author _____

Things about this book/story
that I would be proud of

_____

_____

_____

_____

Things I learned about the
author's style of writing that
I could use in my own writing

_____

_____

_____

_____

Things about this book/story
that I would change

_____

_____

_____

_____

If I were to talk about this
book with a friend, I would
be sure to point out

_____

_____

_____

_____

Quotables

Name _____   Date _____

Book Title _____   Author _____

Skim through your book and search for three quotes that are especially significant. These quotes might be selected because they offer outstanding descriptions, give deeper insight into a character, foreshadow an upcoming problem, represent an important moment in the story, or represent a moment when you personally felt connected to the story or to a character. As you select your quotes, think about how you could explain their importance to someone else.

Quote #1	Why I chose it
_____	_____
_____	_____
_____	_____

Quote #2	Why I chose it
_____	_____
_____	_____
_____	_____

Quote #3	Why I chose it
_____	_____
_____	_____
_____	_____

Assessment of Student's Written Retell

Writer _____

	Retell #1	Retell #2	Retell #3
Date	_____	_____	_____
Text	_____	_____	_____
	Score (1-5)	Score (1-5)	Score (1-5)
Setting	_____	_____	_____
Characters	_____	_____	_____
Complete sequence of events	_____	_____	_____
Problem/Resolution	_____	_____	_____
Relationship to world knowledge	_____	_____	_____
Opinions	_____	_____	_____
Overall Retell	_____	_____	_____

ASSESSMENT
Assessment: Written Retell

Student Name _____   Date _____

Book Title _____   Author _____

This assessment completed by:
☐ the author of this retell   Reviewer _____
☐ peer reviewers
☐ the teacher
☐ the author's parent

	Very detailed		Some details		Not clear
Logical sequence	5	4	3	2	1
Characters	5	4	3	2	1
Character development	5	4	3	2	1
Setting	5	4	3	2	1
The Problem	5	4	3	2	1
The Resolution	5	4	3	2	1
References to the literary devices used by the author	5	4	3	2	1

ASSESSMENT
Collaborative Grading Format

Title of Writing _____   Date _____

Author _____

Student Rating: Circle the number that best describes your opinion.

This piece of writing is: Needs improvement   Excellent
1. Interesting to a reader   1   2   3   4   5

    Justification

2. Descriptive, creating clear
    pictures in the mind of the reader   1   2   3   4   5

    Justification

3. Carefully edited for punctuation
    and spelling   1   2   3   4   5

    Justification

While working on this writing, I learned _____

_____

I deserve the grade of _____ because _____

_____

ASSESSMENT
Collaborative Grading Format

Title of Writing _____ Date _____

Author _____

Teacher Rating:

This piece of writing is: Needs improvement   Excellent

1.   Interesting to a reader   1   2   3   4   5

     Justification

2.   Descriptive, creating clear
     pictures in the mind of the reader   1   2   3   4   5

     Justification

3.   Carefully edited for punctuation
     and spelling   1   2   3   4   5

     Justification

In this piece of writing, I noticed improvement on _____

_____

I believe you deserve the grade of _____ because _____

_____

Parent Page: Writing at Home

Dear Parent(s),

When children write, they learn a lot about reading. They see how words go together and they develop a better understanding of how to communicate.

The writing activity that follows is designed to help children of all ages improve their ability to write descriptively. It can be done with favorite foods you already have in your kitchen, and it should be fun for everyone!

1.   Help your child to select one favorite food item from your kitchen. This might be a marshmallow, a chocolate kiss, a scoop of ice cream, a piece of fruit, a cookie, a breakfast cereal, or something else.

2.   Explain to your child that you are going to use all of your senses to experience this special food (eyes, ears, nose, touch, taste).

3.   Using your eyes: Hold the food item up and really look closely at it. Help your child to describe in detail what he or she sees. Are there wrinkles? Is it smooth? Is there color? As you and your child describe the item, work together to write all of the descriptive words you are using.

4.   Use each of the other senses to continue this descriptive process. Are there any sounds associated with this food? Any smells? When you touch it, what does it feel like? When you taste it slowly, what textures and tastes come to mind?

5.   Assist your child in reading the list of words you have created about this food experience.

6.   We will have a special bulletin board at school waiting to showcase these food explorations. Please have your child draw a picture and then write about this food experience. As your child writes, encourage the use of descriptive words and phrases from the list you created together.

Enjoy!

4

. . . .

Informational Text

Informational text permeates our everyday lives. Newspapers, computer manuals, television directories, maps, cookbooks, and magazines are firmly woven into the texture of our culture. Yet, these are the very texts that learners tell us are the most challenging to them.

To become reflective readers and writers of informational text, readers must have both extensive and intensive experience with information-bearing text. They need to be read to from this genre to deepen their understanding of the language structures of expository material. They need to learn to absorb cues from visual supports such as photographs, charts, diagrams, and boldfaced text (Moline 1995). They need to learn how to activate and utilize their own prior knowledge on the topic and to apply a wide range of metacognitive strategies for making meaning while seeking information.

As we reflect on children as readers of informational text, it becomes apparent that we must aggressively engage them at the earliest stages of literacy development with nonfiction reading. When children read about spiders or ants or magnets, curiosity is stimulated and language flows easily. Informational texts that are predictable and well written provide emergent as well as developing and fluent readers with opportunities to apply their fledgling understandings about print while expanding their world knowledge. They continue to grow as readers and writers and deepen their understanding of a genre that will dominate their learning careers.

Using informational text is particularly helpful to children who are learning English as a second language. The concrete nature of the real world makes it easier for these children to create bridges between their first and second languages. They can see direct linguistic matches when objects or animals are the focus of language learning. A worm is a worm, conceptually, in any language. In narrative text, the challenges are much more complex. Cultural issues and complex concepts such as love and emotion are much more difficult to explain to a language learner. It becomes even more difficult when English language learners are fed a steady diet of narrative texts that feature pigs in skirts and other phenomenon that do not exist in their native culture.

To assist learners in becoming reflective and strategic readers of informational text, it is helpful to remember that reading strategies can be taught in all texts. A science teacher, for example, while teaching about gravity might also utilize the text to support metacognitive strategies such as activating prior knowledge and summarizing. These strategies, often thought of as the domain of reading/language arts teaching, will actually assist the science teacher to reach the goal of helping students understand gravity.

It is also critical to remember the enormous impact prior knowledge has on an individual's ability to make meaning while reading. Even though I consider myself to be a competent reader, I was recently stumped when my son asked me for assistance with a high school passage about coordinate geometry. I was able to say all of the words on the page, even maintain reasonable fluency and intonation, but I could not get a visual image or create even the most shallow of explanations for what I had just read. For the sake of our students, we must remember that "reading" informational text is about concepts and understandings. The more we build upon and connect to prior knowledge, the more the reader will understand and retain. If my son's passage about coordinate geometry had been preceded by an experience with manipulatives, I would have had a much better chance of grasping meaning as I read. It is of significant concern that expository *reading* for many students is often a listening experience. Well-meaning teachers, concerned about textbooks that are too difficult, often create situations where one student reads from the text and others listen or attempt to follow along in the book. This situation does little to build conceptual understandings and can actually deter from the learning process as the "listeners" are engaging in very little reading.

The following visuals, The Teacher and The Reader, provide an overview of teacher and reader behaviors that can directly influence a learner's ability to process informational text and enhance long-term retention of information.

Because informational text is structured differently than narrative, learners benefit from retelling supports, which help them to focus their reflections. The following visuals, Retelling Expository Text and Understanding Text Structure, are designed to assist learners in organizing a retell that is concise, relates new learning to prior knowledge, and acknowledges data gathered from all sources of information.

The Teacher

Before reading

- Engages students in in-depth conversations, demonstrations, and hands-on experience with the concepts dealt in the reading assignment.

- Provides time for students to make predictions about the reading and formulate "I Wonder" questions about the topic.

- Supports the students in identifying good reader strategies such as midstream summarizing, using picture clues, or identifying key points in each section of text.

During reading

- Conferences with readers about their reading strategies as well as the content.

- Ensures that students read silently, with partners, or in unison. Avoids "round robin" reading.

After reading

- Directs students to take time to reflect on the learning and provides time for students to talk and/or write about their understandings.

- Supports students in considering their "I Wonder" questions.

- Debriefs with students about good reader strategies that they feel helped them make meaning and retain information.

- Avoids rote answering of questions and focuses on using the information gained in some meaningful way.

The Reader

Before I read

- I take time to think about what I already know on this topic.

- I look through the pages to think about charts, boldfaced headings, and pictures.

- I ask myself "I Wonder" questions before reading.

While I read

- I stop often to think about what I understand.

- I continue to consider my questions about the topic.

- I use context and all possible clues to get to the meaning of unknown words.

- I try to identify key ideas and concepts.

After I read

- I turn back through the pages and reflect on what I have learned.

- I think about my "I Wonder" questions.

- I use what I have learned by writing or talking about it.

What is the topic?

What are the most important ideas to remember?

What did you learn that you didn't already know?

What is the setting for this information?

What did you notice about the organization and text structure?

What did you notice about the visuals such as graphs, charts, and pictures?

Can you summarize what you learned?

What do you think was the author's purpose for writing this article?

Understanding Text Structure

Name of reader _____

Review an array of textbooks and resource books to see if you can find examples of each structure. See if any structures seem to appear more often than others.

Structure	Number of examples found (tally)	List titles of examples found
Description: Example: The crocodile is the master of deception in water. It stalks its prey and then swiftly closes in for the kill.	_____	_____ _____ _____ _____ _____
Problem/Solution: Example: One problem to resolve in crocodile watching is transportation. How can an observer get close enough to watch without scaring it away or being attacked?	_____	_____ _____ _____ _____ _____ _____
Time/Order: Example: Archaeologists have helped us to understand that the evolution of the crocodile began with . . .	_____	_____ _____ _____ _____ _____ _____

Comparison/Contrast:
Example: The power of the
crocodile is like that
of a monstrous machine.
With one lunge it can
destroy its prey and
protect the kill from
other predators.

_____ _____
_____
_____
_____
_____
_____

Cause/Effect:
Example: We observed the
crocodile as it stalked a
raccoon moving through
the moonlight toward the
edge of the water. As a
result of a noise we made,
the raccoon bolted . . .

_____ _____
_____
_____
_____
_____
_____

Directions:
Example: When observing
a crocodile, first you must . . .

_____ _____
_____
_____
_____

Review a piece of your own informational writing. Which structure did you
use? Have you used any others?

_____

_____

_____

_____

_____

_____

Coaching Session

Informational Text Retell

Group Experience   Assist the students in identifying the text structure of a focus text. You may want to demonstrate this as a think aloud or through activities such as Understanding Text Structure. The goal is to help students understand that a teller may need to vary a retell to match the structure of the text.

Individual Conference   Assist a student to first identify the structure of the text he or she is reading and then take time to look at organization of the writing. How were illustrations/graphs and subheadings used to convey information and highlight important points? As the student plans and executes a retell using both structure and organization appropriate to this text, watch for evidence of the elements of text structure.

Postreading Conference
Debrief the retell with the learner, emphasizing positive uses of the structure and appropriate inclusion of information.

Coaching Session: Informational Retells

Student Name _____ Date _____

Text _____

Observer Notes:

Description:

- Emphasis on key concepts.
- Details to support but not override key concepts.
- Is there enough information to build a visual image?

Problem/Solution:

- Is the problem clearly stated?
- Is there detail included in the solution to the problem?
- What is the importance of this information?

Time/Order:

- Events need to be listed in chronological order.
- Details to support key understandings.

Comparison/Contrast:

- Are the issues being compared clearly stated?
- Are the contrasts and comparisons explained in enough detail to know why this is important?

Cause/Effect:

- What caused what to happen?
- Why is it important?

Directions:

- Details and correct order are essential.

Coding Strategy

This strategy is designed to help students be reflective readers, pausing and weighing what they are reading against their prior knowledge. It also increases the likelihood that students will engage in self-questioning as they read.

Because students need to write their reactions next to what they are reading, it works best to have them read from photocopies. An alternative that saves paper is to have students paper clip one-inch-wide strips of paper down the margin of each page they read or place sticky notes down the side, and then place their "codes" on these pieces of paper.

As students read, their task is to stop at each sentence or each paragraph and indicate their reactions to their reading in the following ways.

* I already knew this!

+ New information

! Wow

?? I don't understand

Think-Pair-Share

At the end of the page or section, students meet in groups and talk about their reactions and understandings. I find it helpful to have students compare their coding with a partner. The social interaction and discussion enriches understanding and provides a forum for reflective engagement. (Remember the VIP strategy from Chapter 1!)

Nonfiction Scaffold

Name _____ Date _____

Topic/Book _____

Before I read I thought _____

_____

After reading more I found _____

_____

Besides this, I learned _____

_____

Finally, I noticed that _____

_____

Create an illustration to show something you learned from your investigation.

A Definition Poem

_____

Name it

_____

Describe it, rename it

_____

Tell where it would be found

_____

Tell more about it

_____

Use emotion words to
tell how you feel about this

_____

Explain why you used
the emotion words on line 5

Example:

Eagle

Our national bird

Soaring near mountains and trees

King of the air

Awesome predator

Respected and feared by all

Focusing on Important Ideas

Reader _____   Text _____

1. Skim headings, charts, and paragraph openings. What does most of the information seem to be about? _____

   _____

2. If there are questions at the end of the chapter, skim them. What are some key points to watch for while reading? _____

   _____

   _____

3. What are some questions of your own on this topic? _____

   _____

   _____

4. Pick a "during reading" strategy such as Coding or VIP to help you get the most from the text.

5. While reading, stop often to think about what you are reading. You might want to look for a summary at the end of each section to help you focus on key ideas.

6. Remember: The goal is to pick the most important information.

7. After reading, stop and think about what you learned.

8. Look at your personal questions. Were they answered? _____

9. Talk to someone about what you learned. You might also want to write, draw, or make a list of key ideas to remember.

10. Think about how you helped yourself be a good reader. What did you do that helped you focus on meaning while reading? _____

   _____

Word Predictions

Reader(s) _____

Focus topic: _____

• Before reading

Preview the text quickly by looking at pictures and other graphic supports. Then *close your book* and work with a partner or a team to list all of the words you think you will encounter in a reading passage about this topic. With each word, tell WHY you think it will appear.

Our words: **(√) appeared during the reading**

_____   _____

_____   _____

_____   _____

_____   _____

_____   _____

_____   _____

• During reading:

Watch for your words to see if they appear in the text.

• After reading:

Go back to your list of words. Put a check next to any words that actually appeared in the reading. Talk to your partners about WHY the others might not have appeared in the reading selection.

Generalization Strategy

Name: _____ Date: _____

Resources used: _____

Student Challenge: Identify the three *most important ideas* in the passage or in your unit of study. Justify your opinions with page numbers, specific points in a text, or with points you have gathered from several sources. The important point is WHY you think these ideas are *more important* than others.

Essential understanding 1: Draw and/or write

Justification: _____

_____

Essential understanding 2: Draw and/or write

Justification: _____

_____

Essential understanding 3: Draw and/or write

Justification: _____

_____

Question-Generating Strategy

1. Preview a text.
    Read titles, subheadings, the table of contents
    Look at pictures or illustrations
    Read the *first paragraph*

2. Think of an "I Wonder" question. Write it down.

    I wonder _____

    _____

3. Read to answer your question. Write the answer when you find it.

    _____

    _____

    _____

4. Ask yourself another "I Wonder" question, then read the next section to find the answer.

    I wonder _____

    _____

5. Continue to read small segments—be sure to ask yourself a question *before* each section.

6. Write or draw to show the most important ideas you learned.

Weaving a Web of Understanding

After taking time to reflect on a topic or an informational text, students gather in a circle. The first student holds a ball of yarn and tells one thing that is remembered about the focus text. While the first student holds onto the end of the string, the ball of yarn is passed across, not around, the circle to another student. This student tells one more thing that is remembered and holds onto the string while passing the ball across the circle to another student. As the ball of yarn continues to be passed, it forms a "web."

If the ball gets to a student who cannot think of a reflection that hasn't already been stated, it is acceptable to repeat an idea.

This works both in a whole class and small-group formats but intensity for individual learners is greater in a small group, as they have more responsibility to share information.

Table of Contents Retell

Select a text and preview the table of contents *before* reading. Have students write questions about each section of the table of contents. Engage the students in searching for answers to their questions by reading the focus text and/or utilizing other resources.

After the reading and researching, ask each student to return to the table of contents and think of at least one thing that was learned regarding each section of the contents page. Move to a paired sharing where students meet in partners and tell each other what they learned about each subtopic listed.

This could be advanced to a collaborative effort by labeling sheets of butcher paper with the subheadings from the contents page and then placing them around the room. Partners or cooperative groups could then move around the room adding their personal collections of evidence to each sheet. The final collections could be typed into a student-authored book on the topic.

Reciprocal Teaching

Adapted from Palincsar and Brown.

Step 1: Take time to help students learn about the four underpinnings of reciprocal teaching and learning. I read an informational text to the students and stop often throughout the reading to model the following processes.

• *Predict.* What do you think the next section is going to be about? What information might be included?

• *Clarify.* What did the author mean when he or she said _____? What does the word _____ mean on page _____?

• *Ask yourself questions.* What were the important ideas?

• Orally *summarize* the reading. State main ideas and important details up to this point in the reading.

Step 2: After several think aloud experiences with the process, students are ready to continue the process in small groups. The teacher is a member of the group and takes a turn as group leader, just as the students do. Reading segments are kept short so that the students can work together to negotiate meaning in manageable chunks. The group leader reads the cards shown on page 139, one at a time, and guides the discussion.

The cards are passed to the next group member and the process is repeated with the next segment of reading and a new group leader.

Reciprocal Teaching Cards

To use before each section.

Card #1. "Please get ready to read to _____." (Select a boldfaced heading or an apparent stopping point in the text.)	Card #2. "I predict this section will be about _____." (Discussion leader speaks.)
Card #3. "Does anyone else have a prediction?" (Encourage group members to speak.)	Card #4. "Please read silently to the point we selected."

To use after reading each section:

Card #5. "Are there any words you thought were interesting?" (Invite group members to speak.)	Card #6. "Are there any ideas you found interesting or puzzling?" (Invite group members to contribute.)
Card #7. "Do you have comments about the reading?" (Group response.)	Card #8. "Summarize (in 2 or 3 sentences): This was about _____." (Discussion leader.)

Pass the cards to the new leader.

Read, Cover, Remember, and Retell

Unfortunately, some learners will continue reading even if they aren't understanding the material. The Read, Cover, Remember, and Retell process supports readers by stopping them frequently to THINK about the meaning. Students tell us that this strategy is very helpful during standardized testing. Thanks to Jan Ellison, Title I teacher, Beaverton, OR.

READ only as much as your hand can cover.

COVER the words with your hand.

REMEMBER what you have just read. (It is OK to take another look.)

RETELL what you just read inside your head or to a partner.

Investigations

Knowing that we live in an information age where we can no longer expect to master all knowledge, we must recognize that the most important issue is teaching readers and writers how to *find* information when they need it and then how to *present* it in a way that is usable and comprehensible to others.

Investigations are short probes into a topic. The student selects the topic, engages in brief research, and then presents the work both visually and orally.

A final form needs to have:

- **a title**
- **a diagram or map**
- **a border related to the topic**
- **a layout that measures 11" x 17"**
- **neatly written paragraphs**

FIGURE 4–1   Jeremy's T-Rex investigation

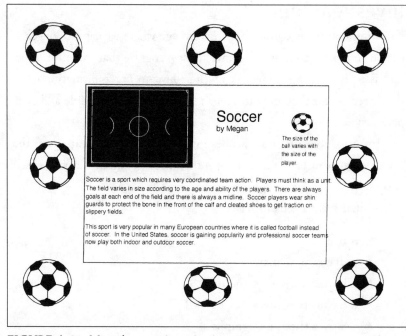

FIGURE 4–2   Megan's soccer investigation

My Investigation

Name _____ Date _____

My Topic _____

Important facts I have learned _____

_____

_____

I will include a map or diagram of _____

My drawings will be _____

My border will be _____

Rough Sketch of Investigation

Read and Retell

The Procedure

1. Predict: Photocopy a page of text and fold it so that only the title is showing.

    Have the students predict the genre and/or the plot.

    Write the predictions.

    Share with the group/justify predictions.

2. Predict Words: List words that might occur in the reading. Share and compare with the group.

3. Read and reread if desired.

4. Write a summary on the back of the photocopy of the text. Write it for someone who has not read the story and needs to hear as much as possible. Do not look back to the story.

5. Share and Compare. Work with a group or a partner to consider: What did I include or omit that is different from yours? Why did you omit this part that I have? Do you think I changed or omitted anything that is important?

6. Paraphrase Power: Ask your partners if you used any words/phrases that are different from the story but still mean the same thing.

7. Borrow a bit. Ask your partner: If you could take a bit of my retelling and include it in yours, which bit would you take? Why?

8. Group Share: Reflect on the process and which strategies seemed to help.

Fact or Fib?

This one is fun, a stretch for understanding, and a great way for students to celebrate the efforts of their peers! Students utilize this strategy to reflect upon a unit of study, a favorite literature selection, or a current event.

1. Have them make a list of facts that they remember.

2. For each fact, they need to decide if they will write the answer as a fact or a fib. For example:

    Statement: "Bat wings have skin on them." Fact or Fib?

    Answer: "Fact. They have thin, flexible skin, not feathers."

3. The students enjoy folding 5 x 7 cards in half, writing their statement on the front and their answers inside.

Read and Retell adapted from Brown and Cambourne 1987.
Fact or Fib?: Thanks to Jodi Wilson, educational consultant.

Reflecting on Main Ideas

Use this chart to retell the key points for a partner or your family.

Name _____ Date _____

Book _____

Page Number	Select One Main Idea	Most Important Details (Choose one or two)

Word Sorts

Prereading word sorts offer students an opportunity to activate prior knowledge and topic-related vocabulary. The kinesthetic and visual nature of this structure keeps the attention of even the most challenged learners.

The teacher:

- Selects words and phrases from a text or a topic of study and prepares a word sort (see the sample below and on page 25).
- Assists students through demonstrations and think alouds to understand the process of looking for relationships.
- Engages the students both during and after reading in adjusting their understandings on the topic.

The students:

- Work in teams to separate the words.
- Arrange the words in the following ways:
  1. Pairs of words that "go together." For example, talons prey. The students then think of a sentence using the words. Example: "Eagles use their talons to capture their prey."
  2. Categories of words that "go together." For example, broad wings talons strong beak. The students tell why they think these go together. Example: "These are all body parts of an eagle."
- Make a list: What other words do you think might be included in a text on this topic?
- Share their understandings and word predictions with other groups.
- Read the text or resources, searching for confirmation of their predictions about relationships and presence of their predicted words.
- Review the words after reading to see if their new understandings lead to new statements.

Sample for eagles:

broad wings	talons	predators	wild
nests	national bird	no enemies	forty years
meat	strong beak	good eyesight	bald
respected	wilderness	fish	prey

Alliteration Fun

Poetic formats add variety to informational learning. They also stimulate visual images, which can enhance long-term learning and enhance descriptive writing.

The Process   Students write three word clusters that describe a topic. All words must start with the same letter. The clusters then form an informational poem.

Apples

Crisp, crunchy, crackly apples
Round, red, rotten apples
Smelly, smooth, succulent apples
Apples

Alliteration Fun

_____

The topic

_____ , _____ , _____ , _____

the topic

_____ , _____ , _____ , _____

the topic

_____ , _____ , _____ , _____

the topic

_____

the topic

Alpha Antics

Students reflect on what they have learned about a topic and then begin listing words that reflect their understanding.

For example, while studying about eagles, students might decide that *wingspan, protected status,* and *eyesight* are critical understandings. Using the format on page 150, they might write:

W is for eagle. Because they can have up to an eight-foot *wingspan.*

P is for eagle. Because eagles are *protected* by law.

E is for eagle. Because eagles have incredible *eyesight* and can see much better at a distance than a human.

Example for snow:

M is for snowman. Because eventually all snowmen *melt.*

Example for worms:

FIGURE 4–3 Alpha Antics

Alpha Antics: _____
Topic

_____ is for _____

Because _____

_____

_____ is for _____

Because _____

_____

_____ is for _____

Because _____

_____

Illustration

Research Plan: _____
Topic

Name _____ Date _____

I am very interested in learning more about _____

_____

I already know that _____

_____

_____

To gather more information I will use _____

_____

I will present my information in the form of (oral presentation, display, report, readers theater script, song, student-authored book, or something else). _____

I expect to be finished by _____

My Action Plan: Steps to Success

First I will _____

Then I will _____

After that I plan to _____

Finally, I will _____

to demonstrate what I have learned.

Dictionaries

Dictionaries are a wonderful structure that invite students to revisit recent topics or favorite literature selections while developing a deeper understanding of a genre (dictionaries) they will use throughout life. To create a dictionary, students make lists of all the words they can think of that relate to a certain topic. They then write definitions for each of the words on half sheets of paper. (Be sure to have them revise for content and edit for conventions.) The next step is to put the definitions in alphabetical order and decide how many words will go on each page, as well as which ones should be illustrated. The last step is to insert guide words at the top of each page. More proficient readers and writers might even want to divide their words into syllables!

On a topic:

Reflecting on a book:

The Soccer Dictionary

Field   Goal

<u>Field</u>. A grass area where you play soccer.

<u>Flags</u>. When the ball has gone out of bounds, the flag is raised.

<u>Forward</u>. A person who waits at center field then dribbles the ball up to the goal.

<u>Goal</u>. The place you kick the ball.

Faithful Elephants

A Thoughtful Dictionary

Snakes   Syringe

<u>Snakes</u>. The snakes died quickly. They did not suffer.

<u>Stop</u>. The zookeepers wanted the war to stop.

<u>Survive</u>. The elephants tried not to die.

<u>Syringe</u>. A needle used for injections.

SOCCER

Assistant coach   **Cheering**

Assistant Coach. The person who is second in charge of the team.

Athletic Bag. A bag that you carry your soccer things in.

Back pass. A pass that you make to someone who is behind you

Bad Weather. A rainy and muddy day.

Bodyblock. Blocking the ball with your body

Captain. A person who goes to the coin toss.

Center Circle. A circle that is in the middle of the field.

Chalk. It is around the field.

Cheering. People who stand on the sidelines and scream.

FIGURE 4–4 The Soccer Dictionary

Book Review: Nonfiction

Name _____   Date _____

Title of Book _____   Author _____

What was your opinion of this book?

What did the author do especially well?

What could the author have improved in the book?

What did you learn that was especially interesting?

How did the author use visuals such as graphs, photographs, charts to explain the topic?

What did you learn about the craft of informational writing?

What techniques can you apply in your own writing?

Informational Book Rating

Name _____   Date _____

Name of Book _____

Author _____   Illustrator _____

		Outstanding	OK	Not so great		
1.	The author made the information easy to understand.	5	4	3	2	1
2.	The writing style was comfortable to read.	5	4	3	2	1
3.	The book was organized in a logical way.	5	4	3	2	1
4.	The author explained ideas completely before shifting topics.	5	4	3	2	1
5.	The charts, graphs, and pictures were helpful.	5	4	3	2	1
6.	The table of contents and index were organized and easy to use.	5	4	3	2	1
7.	My overall rating of this book is	5	4	3	2	1

Comments:

Project Self-Reflection: _____

Topic

Name _____ Date _____

As I think about the research project I have just completed, I am especially pleased about _____

_____

I think this turned out so well because _____

_____

The most important thing I learned while working on this project was _____

_____

If I were to improve one thing about my project, I would _____

_____

My next goal is _____

_____

Assessment: Self-Evaluation

Oral Presentation of Research

Name _____ Date _____

Topic _____

	Working on it	OK		Great

My Research

1. I used resources. 1 2 3 4 5
2. I took notes and organized
   ideas. 1 2 3 4 5
3. I prepared visuals for
   my audience. 1 2 3 4 5

My Presentation

1. I spoke clearly so everyone
   could hear. 1 2 3 4 5
2. I maintained eye contact with
   the audience. 1 2 3 4 5
3. I made it interesting to the
   audience. 1 2 3 4 5
4. I presented it in an order that
   made sense. 1 2 3 4 5

I was best at _____

_____

I would like to improve _____

_____

_____

Observation Guide:
Reading of Informational Text

Student _____ Date _____

Assessment completed by _____

1. As the student previewed the
    pictures, the information gathered was   minimal   substantial

            1   2   3   4   5

2. In a one-on-one conference,
    the student read the material   word by word   smoothly

            1   2   3   4   5

3. The student used a variety of
    strategies for unknown words   used only one   used multiple
                                    strategy   strategies

            1   2   3   4   5

4. The reader's miscues maintained
    meaning   rarely   most of the time

            1   2   3   4   5

5. The reader self-corrected when
    meaning broke down   rarely   most of the time

            1   2   3   4   5

6. The reader cross-checked with
    grapho-phonic cues   rarely   most of the time

            1   2   3   4   5

7. The reader provided a retell
    that encompassed key concepts
    and did not dwell on lesser details   inadequate attempt very complete retell

            1   2   3   4   5

8. The reader can describe
    strategies for making meaning
    in informational text   has few   describes multiple
                                    strategies   strategies

            1   2   3   4   5

Observation Guide:
Writing of Informational Text

Student _____ Date _____

Assessment completed by _____

1. The writing shows understanding
   of the topic.

limited			substantial	
understanding			understanding	
1	2	3	4	5

2. The writing is organized in a
   logical way.

not organized			well organized	
1	2	3	4	5

3. There are visuals to support the
   written text.

no visuals			good visuals	
1	2	3	4	5

4. The layout of the writing and visuals
   is visually appealing.

little evidence of effort			well laid out	
1	2	3	4	5

5. There is an emphasis on key concepts
   in this writing.

details only			substantial concepts	
1	2	3	4	5

6. Details are used to support key concepts
   and do not dominate the writing.

too many details			well done	
1	2	3	4	5

7. Descriptions are adequate for a reader
   to create visual images while reading.

few descriptors			many descriptors	
1	2	3	4	5

8. Conventions such as punctuation and
   spelling have been adequately addressed.

needs assistance			well done	
1	2	3	4	5

9. The writer understands the steps of
   gathering information, planning,
   writing, revising, and editing.

limited understanding			right on!	
1	2	3	4	5

10. The writer's voice was evident in this
    writing.

not present			strongly felt	
1	2	3	4	5

During Reading Strategy Observation

As you conference with students who are reading expository text, indicate which strategies are being used.

The Reader _____   Date _____

The Book _____

The Reader:	Strategy observed	Notes
Uses the table of contents	☐	
Skims through the text before reading	☐	
During reading pauses to use pictures, graphs, etc.	☐	
Uses the index or glossary if needed	☐	
Uses titles, subheadings, bold print	☐	
Varies reading rate to match the demands of the text	☐	
Rereads to confirm understanding	☐	
Uses context clues to derive meaning for unknown words	☐	
Substitutes synonyms for unknown words to attempt to maintain meaning	☐	
Self-corrects when meaning breaks down	☐	

Overall rating:
How effectively did the student uses the above strategies while reading?

	still needs assistance		very effective use	
1	2	3	4	5

ASSESSMENT
Project Evaluation

Name _____ Date _____

Project _____

Team Members _____

	Student Rating	Teacher Rating
Quality of Ideas Key concepts and conclusions are clearly expressed	1 2 3 4 5	1 2 3 4 5
Expression of Ideas A variety of communication tools are used (writing, illustrations, maps, graphs, models, etc.)	1 2 3 4 5	1 2 3 4 5
Creativity Visually interesting, use of unusual media or forms of communicating	1 2 3 4 5	1 2 3 4 5
Conventions Conventional spelling, punctuation, grammar, effort in editing, looks polished	1 2 3 4 5	1 2 3 4 5
Oral Presentation Organized, audible, clearly explained	1 2 3 4 5	1 2 3 4 5
Participation All members shared in the work	1 2 3 4 5	1 2 3 4 5

Comments: _____

_____

Parent Page: Interactive Assessment

Have your students select an example of informational learning to celebrate. The chosen item can be a project, a piece of art, a piece of writing, and so forth. The student then is responsible to write on the form on page 163: "I am proud of this because." The teacher adds a positive celebration in the middle section and then the work goes home for the parent to add a positive comment in the last section. The comment sheet and the work come back to school and can be shared through private conferences with the teacher, through group sharing sessions, or considered as a portfolio addition.

It can be especialy meaningful if this is done monthly so the parents get used to focusing on positive points in student work samples.

Monthly examples can also be kept together so parents can reflect each month on progress made since the beginning of the year.

Interactive Assessment Form

Date _____

Student

I am proud of this because _____

_____

_____

Teacher

I am proud of this because _____

_____

_____

Parent

I am proud of this because _____

_____

_____

5

. . . .

The Arts
Powerful Tools for Enhancing Understanding

Drama and the visual arts were once saved for enrichment—reserved for the highest functioning students or for occasional breaks from the serious work of reading and writing. We know, however, that experiences with the arts allow learners to actually deepen and expand their understandings (Hoyt 1992). When learners have opportunities to translate their knowledge into clay, paint, or drama, they must examine the details of their knowledge and develop a new perspective from the role of artist. Learners must generate new meanings and consciously apply the information through the artistic medium. Harste, Short, and Burke (1988) describe this processes as *transmediation.*

To apply these understandings in a literacy-learning environment, students need to engage with the arts in combination with rigorous reading and writing experiences. This isn't to suggest a romantic view of literacy, but rather one that actively implements the newest research on the brain (Nash 1997). We now know that experiences with music, visual stimulation (such as art), physical activity, and other forms of sensory input cause increases in electrical activity within the brain. The arts are powerful tools.

Comprehension cannot be fostered by transmitting information from the page into the children's heads. Learning occurs when one creates a personal interpretation. This interpretation can take the form of a feeling, an artistic expression, or a rush of language as the individual makes a connection to the information. Each learner personalizes and internalizes in different ways.

We need to help learners activate their senses, their imaginations, their emotions, and all their life experiences while interacting with text. With the support of multiple communication systems, even learners with special needs can bring life into the words on the page.

Lesson Planning

When I am planning literacy experiences, I use a process that helps me ensure that I'm providing a balance of learning experiences. Using a format similar to the one shown here, I simply check that children are utilizing reading, writing, conversation, and some artistic experience in each learning opportunity.

Book _____   ☐ Reading

                                                   Strategy focus _____

                                                   ☐ Writing

                                                   Strategy focus _____

                                                   ☐ Conversation

                                                   ☐ Artistic experience

As a result students learning about elephants are very likely to read elephant books, write elephant stories, create elephants out of clay, dramatize the movements of an elephant, and do lots of talking about what they are learning.

Dramatic Reflections

Drama evokes higher order thinking, problem solving, feeling, and language use as students strive to demonstrate their knowledge orally (Booth 1987). The children invent most of the dialogue and action, drawing ideas from the environment, their reading, and their background knowledge. They use their bodies and their voices as ways of communicating their understandings. Transmediation occurs are they translate their knowledge into motion and verbal interpretation.

In whole-class dramatics, students might respond to a shared book experience or a read aloud by retelling their understandings through body motions and appropriate sound effects. They can sensitize their bodies to the descriptors used in a story as they really feel the sun beating on their skin or the icy wind forcing them back from the edge of a cliff. Visualizations of particular scenes from literature or history can be enhanced by encouraging the students to spontaneously take roles of the characters (Hoyt 1992).

In schools where students have had extensive experience with drama, halls and corners of classrooms are often filled with small groups of children dramatizing favorite literature selections. Using literature or nonfiction as a stimulus, actors dramatize animatedly as the readers move through the text. For the most part, groups have no audience. They find joy in dramatizing a story within their group, just as young children find joy in imaginary play with a friend. There is little evidence of self-consciousness as children use their bodies and their imaginations to deepen their understandings.

Children engaging in dramatic reflection of stories are able to transfer their sense of character role and point of view easily. Youngsters dramatizing *Stone Soup* realized a need for a group of townspeople. Without any specific leadership, they spontaneously gathered as townspeople, then moved back into their individual roles naturally. In addition to expanding their understanding of text and enhancing reflection, these children were engaging in communication, problem solving, and interactive group processes (Hoyt 1990).

The teacher can assist a group by working as a coach. As in conferences for writing (Graves 1982), visits to groups are brief. The teacher's role is to support the children's interactions not to direct them. The coach might offer ideas to individual children, serve as a reader, or assist actors in relating to the story line.

After dramatic interactions, students can be encouraged to re-create a story with pictures or writing. These retellings often reflect powerful new understandings of the story and are punctuated with specific details of the setting and mood. Furthermore, because of the dramatic interaction that preceded the retelling, conversations and written retells are far more sophisticated than they would have been without benefit of the dramatic experience.

Dramatic reflections can be especially successful with learning disabled students and second language learners. The combination of drama, body movement, and discussion lays a strong foundation for story understanding and helps these special learners to verify their information through several communication systems before committing it to writing.

Videotapes are excellent forums for dramatic reflections. Students really enjoy taping their dramatic retells or their book reviews and then showing the tapes to others.

Guess What?

Guess What? is a structure where students use a charades-style format, acting out scenes from well-known stories while the audience guesses the book, the event, the characters.

Word Theater

In Word Theater, readers work in teams of two or three to reflect on a text they have just read in their literature circles. They select three or four words that they found to be particularly interesting in their reading and record them on the form.

It is important to note the page number so they can easily return to the context in which the word occurred.

After listing their words and page numbers, the readers challenge themselves to dramatize the words in such a way that observers can guess their words. When the teams are ready, they direct their observers to turn to the page in the text where their word appears. The observers watch the dramatization of the word then skim the page to try to locate what they believe to be the target word. When the observers believe they have found it, they read the entire sentence in which the word appeared. The dramatic team then confirms or clarifies the guess made by the observers.

Word Theater

Actors _____   The Book _____

Focus word	Selected from page	Plan for dramatizing
1. _____	_____	_____
		_____
		_____
		_____
2. _____	_____	_____
		_____
		_____
		_____
3. _____	_____	_____
		_____
		_____
		_____
4. _____	_____	_____
		_____
		_____
		_____

Expressive, Rehearsed Oral Reading

When readers treat reading as a performance, including dramatic voices, changes in intonation, and perhaps even some soft background music, they are reflecting on and interpreting the story. Students who are given an opportunity to rehearse their reading for a performance must consider voices to represent characters, experiment with tonal quality to match mood, and adjust rate to match rising and falling action of the story. By preparing an interpretation of the story for an audience, readers are engaging in powerful processes that delve deeply into meaning.

To support expressive, rehearsed oral reading, you might consider:

- Demonstrating dramatic reading with soft background music.
- Demonstrating voice changes between characters.
- Demonstrating rate changes and intonation changes to match the story line.
- Wearing a costume or using props to enhance the dramatic reading.
- Inviting students to practice using a tape recorder or a video camera to fine-tune their presentation.

It can seem especially important to the dramatic reader if you advertise in advance that a particular story will be performed on a given day and then make a formal introduction of the dramatic reader at the beginning of the performance.

After the performance is a wonderful opportunity for the audience to provide positive feedback and ask questions of the dramatic reader.

Readers Theater

Unlike drama, in which body motion portrays a great deal of the meaning, readers theater is dependent on the ability of the reader's voice to capture the listener. The readers have the task of using reading rate, intonation, and emphasis on the meaning-bearing cadences of language to make the print come alive.

Readers theater interrelates all aspects of language learning and calls for transmediation as the printed text is translated into expressive oral reading.

The teacher's role is to model expressive reading, assist the students as they experiment with different intonations and reading rates, and support students who may have difficulty. It is important to monitor comprehension through retellings of the readers theater selections so that students are not engaged in rehearsing text that carries little or no meaning for them.

While there are many readers theater scripts available for purchase,

I find the best success with student-authored scripts or teaching students to present their performances straight from the original text. With rehearsal, even emergent readers can read from the quotation marks and indicate whether the speaker is the narrator or a story character.

The Visual Arts

The visual arts are powerful motivators for children. They offer alternative ways for children to express their understanding and to explore their own inner language. Because the study of literacy is too often focused on words, it is important to look back to the images and feelings that precede the words, to explore the relationships between the way children see the world and the way it is interpreted in print. In particular, children who have difficulty with written and oral language may find that artistic expression focused on a learning experience can help them to organize thinking and rehearse for more traditional means of expression.

To draw a picture about a story, learners must draw upon both the affective and the cognitive domains. They must think about all of the story events before selecting one that merits further attention. The event must then be analyzed for elements of setting, characterization, and details before a picture can be drawn. A seemingly simple task actually requires a great deal of evaluation and analysis. The picture also provides a focus for writing. When children draw before they write, the writing tends to stay focused and often includes more detail than writing, which occurs without benefit of drawing.

Many students enjoy illustrating through paint, chalk, and other media. To capitalize on this, I often have groups of students integrate art into their novel studies. Students can take turns painting a picture about a chapter then going to the computer to write a summary. These paintings and summaries can then be mounted as a wall story, which provides an invitation to review previous chapters as the novel continues to unfold. Students also can bind the pages together into a student-authored big book and present it to a class of younger students as an invitation to turn the same novel into a read aloud experience.

While artistic experiences related to text should not significantly reduce the amount of time spent with acts of reading and writing, they can be powerful vehicles for learning.

Picture It!

Invite students to draw several pictures reflecting their thoughts about a shared text. Readers then meet with partners or small groups to talk about the pictures they drew.

Conversation topics might include:

Why did you draw these particular pictures in response to the text?

How are these ideas related to the story?

What order might these pictures be placed in to reflect the text?

Did you think of any experiences in your own life when you were creating these pictures?

Which of your pictures do you think the author would choose as a representation of his or her book?

If you could only choose one picture to use in telling someone else about the story, which one would you choose? Why?

Which of your pictures provide the most information about story elements such as characters, setting, problem, solution?

Variations

For writing   This experience could easily lead into a written reflection about the text by adding print to the illustrations.

For chapter books   At the end of a cluster of chapters, students can gather in groups and create Picture It! summarizations of their reflections up to this point. At the end of each chapter, one student might volunteer to paint an illustration reflecting a key point in the chapter. A brief summary could be developed on the computer and attached to the painting. As the chapters are read, the illustrations and chapter summaries could be placed on the wall and reviewed daily to assist students in reflecting on the unfolding story line.

Note: This procedure can be especially helpful to English language learners and students with a need for language stimulation. The mediation between art and oral language provide a strong foundation for language development.

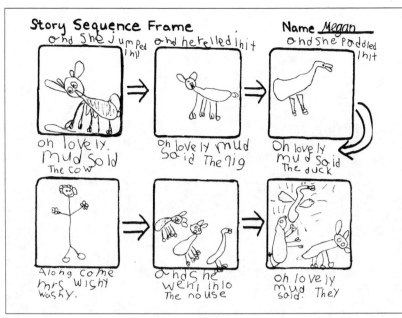

FIGURE 5–1 Megan's story sequence frame

Picture It!

Focus Book _____ Date _____

Name of student illustrator for Picture It! _____

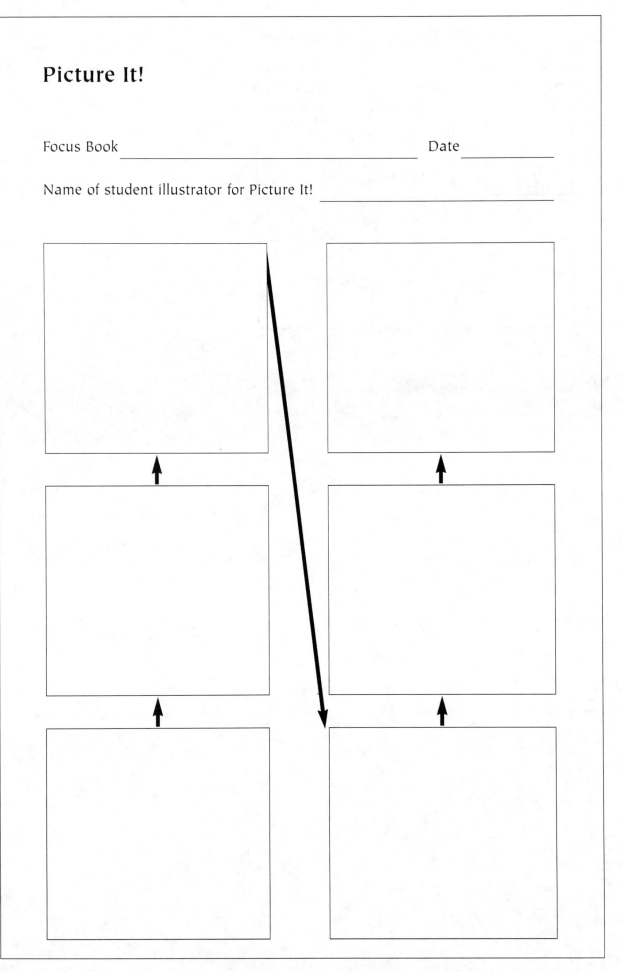

Draw All About It

Format 1

Students work in teams of three or four. Each group selects a storyteller who will be responsible to begin drawing images from the story to assist the other team members in recalling key events from the reading, in the order in which they occurred. The storyteller is not allowed to talk.

The drawings can be on butcher paper, on regular drawing paper, or another kind of paper. It does seem to work best if the storytellers draw with felt pens or pencils so they can focus on illustrating key ideas rather than being distracted by color changes and details.

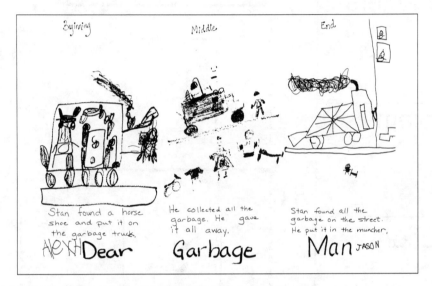

FIGURE 5–2 Dear Garbage Man (Thanks to Claudia Larison.)

Format 2

The storyteller's task is to draw clues to elicit the naming of structural elements such as characters, setting, three key events, problem, and solution. The team needs to review the story in advance and reach agreements about which events are central to the plot.

Draw All About It: 2

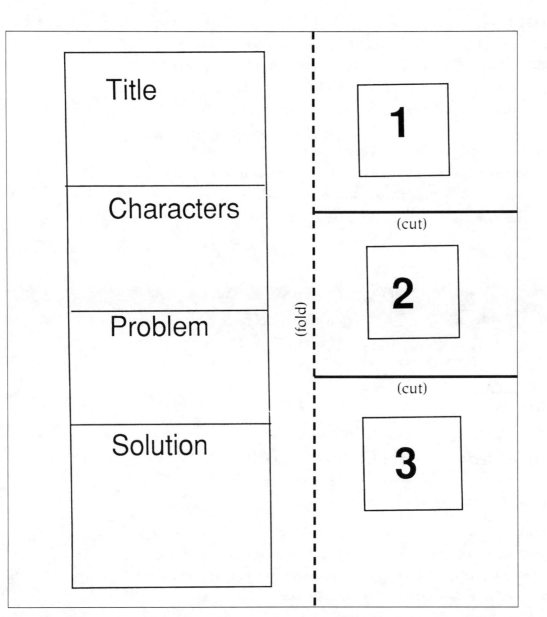

Title

Characters

Problem

Solution

(fold)

1

(cut)

2

(cut)

3

Sketch to Stretch

Students read and/or listen to a selection, then create a sketch related to their reading. It is helpful to demonstrate this first so that students understand that the goal is to create a general image rather than focusing on small details. During the demonstration, a think aloud technique helps students to see how you reflect on the entire story, then pull points together into your quick sketch.

It is also helpful to have students use pencils to sketch so the emphasis is on collecting thoughts rather than on artistic competence. A timer helps as well so that students understand this is a moment to quickly collect their thoughts about the story using a "doodling" technique.

Some students benefit from being asked an open-ended question such as: What did you learn? What did this mean to you? What did it make you think about? What key ideas stayed with you? or What did you think was the most significant part of the story?

After sketching, students share and explain their drawings in small groups. Their sharing should focus on why they drew what they did and what they attempted to represent. The verbal explanation and the resulting conversations are more important to extending understanding than the sketch. The sketch is a vehicle for collecting thoughts and rehearsing for the conversation.

This strategy is especially powerful for students who may be challenged with literacy learning as it provides much-needed quiet time. The drawing provides a quiet atmosphere during which all students can collect their thoughts about their reading and increases likelihood that all can be a contributor to the discussion.

After sharing within groups, each group can select a sketch to share with the whole group or focus on a unifying theme that was present in all of their sketches.

The role of the teacher

- Demonstrate the process.
- Be a partner, doing a sketch and talking about it.
- Encourage students to talk about their reactions to their reading.
- Stimulate conversation about personal meanings they have constructed related to the reading.

This strategy works well with all genres. In addition to high quality literature, you may want to consider using current events in the newspaper, poetry, literature, science experiments, concepts in social studies, health, math, or as a prewriting experience.

Adapted from M. Seigel (1984).

An Artful Reflection for _____

Story

The Artist/Writers _____ Date _____

Beginning Illustration	Middle Illustration	End Illustration

Write about each picture.

_____	_____	_____
_____	_____	_____
_____	_____	_____
_____	_____	_____
_____	_____	_____
_____	_____	_____
_____	_____	_____
_____	_____	_____
_____	_____	_____

Making New Book Jackets

When children look at the book jackets that are made for hardbound books, they often get creative ideas that are perfect formats for retelling.

Many students enjoy making a book jacket for a favorite book. The jacket has a summary, a bit of information about the author when available, and an illustration for the cover.

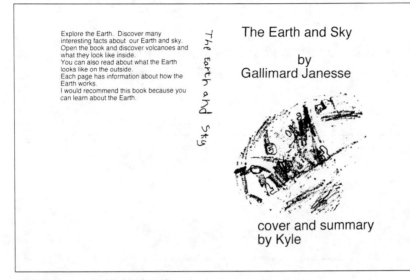

FIGURE 5–4 Kyle's book jacket

Communicating Through Art

Artist _____ Date _____

Book _____

Draw about the story and be ready to tell someone what you know. Later, you can cut these pictures apart, paste each one on a piece of paper, and then write about the pictures.

First

Then

Also

Finally

Puppeteering and Flannelgraphs

There are so many tried-and-true ways to use puppets and flannelgraphs in retells.

Sock puppets

Paper puppets

Fabric puppets

Paper plate puppets

Hand puppets

Characters on flannel or vellum

When students are invited to consider the options, design their own puppets, and write a script for the retell, they can implement knowledge of story, language, physical motion, and art all together.

An additional option to consider   Draw a character from a story, cut around it, attach it to a band that is just large enough to go around your hand. While retelling a story, wear this puppet on your hand.

Filmstrip Art

Thanks to a very creative media specialist, I learned that students could take old filmstrip material, clean it in a mild solution of bleach and water, and then "draw" on the surface to create their own filmstrips. When I introduced this idea to children, they very quickly caught on and began producing filmstrips. This process worked very well for both narrative and expository texts. As I have continued to explore this media form, I have discovered that students can cut overhead transparencies into strips and present their "filmstrips" on the overhead. For many students, the intensity of drawing tiny pictures and doing an oral presentation provided an outstanding foundation for the writing that followed.

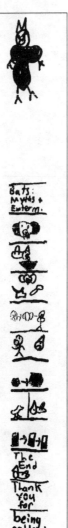

FIGURE 5–5   BATS Filmstrip art

Artful Equations

Invite students to turn characters, problems, and solutions into artful equations.

Cinderella could turn into:

Cleaning girl   +   Fairy Godmother   =   Princess

Create an illustration for each part of the equation.

Artful Equations

The Book _____

The Artist _____

           +   =

           +   =

These equations match the book because _____

_____

_____

Music

Life is full of rhythm. The rolling of the tires on our cars, the sound of the clothes dryer spinning 'round and 'round, the cadences of our language. I once heard Shelley Harwayne at a conference state that "singing is like cursive talking!"

Children love music. They love to sing, to dance, to move to the beat. For some, music is so important to them that they stay more calm and think more clearly when there is soft music playing in the background.

To take advantage of this natural inclination toward music, I use music and rhythm as foundations for reflection and retelling. For reflections, I often turn on soft music, dim the lights, and ask the students to think about what they just learned in math, in science, or some thought to savor from a read aloud story. It is also very powerful to play music in the background while a student performs a retell and points out special points in the illustrations.

Songs can form really exciting structures for retelling. Students can use traditional tunes and write innovations that retell stories. Here's such an example from first-grade students who read *The Enormous Watermelon* retold by Brenda Parkes and Judith Smith:

To the tune of "Here We Go 'Round the Mulberry Bush"

Old Mother Hubbard planted a seed, planted a seed, planted
　　a seed.
Old Mother Hubbard planted a seed.
She wanted a watermelon.

It grew and grew until it was big, until it was big, until it was
　　big.
It grew and grew until it was big.
It soon became enormous!

She tried and tried but couldn't pull it up, couldn't pull it up,
　　couldn't pull it up.
She tried and tried but couldn't pull it up,
So she called on Humpty Dumpty

and so on.

The students wrote the following song as part of a unit on plants. They planted pumpkin seeds, observed their growth, and wrote this song as a retell of their learning.

To the tune of "The Farmer in the Dell"

First you buy some seeds
Oh, first you buy some seeds
Hi Ho the Derry O
First you buy some seeds

You put them in the ground
You put them in the ground
Hi Ho the Derry O
You put them in the ground

You pour on some water
You pour on some water
Hi Ho the Derry O
You pour on some water

The roots begin to grow
The roots begin to grow
Hi Ho the Derry O
The roots begin to grow

The stem comes to the top
The stem comes to the top
Hi Ho the Derry O
The stem comes to the top

The leaves open up
The leaves open up
Hi Ho the Derry O
The leaves open up

After reading *The Piggybook* by Anthony Browne, students wrote the following song:

To the tune of "Mary Had a Little Lamb"

Simon was a little pig, little pig, little pig
Simon was a little pig
He didn't clean his room

Writers in Writers Workshop wrote the following song as a reflection on the rules of punctuation they were learning.

To the tune of "Clementine (Oh My Darling)"
Punctuation Song

Names and places, beginning of sentences
All deserve a capital
Periods come at ends of sentences or abbreviations.

Commas are a little harder
They can leave us feeling blue
They are used in a greeting, in a list or with a phrase.

Punctuation, Punctuation
We are trying hard to learn
These rules can make us crazy
But with patience we can learn.

Traditional Tunes for Retellings

Down in the Meadow
Did You Ever See a Lassie?
Frere Jacque: Are You Sleeping?
Happy Birthday
Home on the Range
I'm a Little Teapot
If You're Happy and You Know It
Itsy Bitsy Spider
London Bridge Is Falling Down
Mary Had a Little Lamb
She'll Be Coming Around the Mountain
Here We Go 'Round the Mulberry Bush
Pop Goes the Weasel
Row, Row, Row Your Boat
Sing a Song of Six Pence
Skip to My Lou
The Farmer in the Dell
The Muffin Man
This Old Man
Twinkle, Twinkle Little Star
Yankee Doodle
Clementine
Somewhere over the Rainbow
On Top of Old Smokey
This Is the Way We Wash Our Clothes
Jingle Bells

Rap

Rap can also provide a wonderful scaffold for retells. Students enjoy using rhythm and rap-style phrasing (without the bad words) to retell both narrative and expository texts and experiences. I find that even the most reluctant writers enjoy this format and gladly engage in lots of revisions to make their phrasing match the rhythm they select.

To use rap as a follow-up to a reading experience:

- Have the students retell a familiar story and record the events of the story on sentence strips.
- Hang the sentences in a pocket chart so they are clearly visible.
- Rewrite each sentence using "rap" style.
- Find some music for background, work out a clapping rhythm, or use a keyboard with background rhythms to accompany the reading.

Goldilocks Rap
Written by sixth graders

Once upon a time there were three dudes.
They be-bopped through the woods while their oatmeal cooled.
Along came a chick named Goldilocks.
She went slipping and sliding into the awesome house
She gulped down some porridge
She trashed the chair
She slipped upstairs and no one was there
She dozed off on the rock 'n roll bed
And woke up when the three dudes said
"Come back again you sleepy head"
That's all, that's all . . . there ain't no more
This is the end my sweet little friend.

Thomas' Snowsuit
By Robert Munsch, retold by third graders

Thomas was a really bad dude
Who didn't like his suit
He drove his mom crazy and his teacher insane
When he wouldn't put on that suit

They called in the principal to get the job done
But much to his surprise
He ended up in the teacher's dress
And it wasn't even his size!

To use rap for fun or to capture an important idea from a content area:

- Brainstorm important issues.
- Experiment with word clusters or webs to stimulate related vocabulary.

And then start writing!

Here's an example by fourth graders:

Dolphins, Porpoises, Whales, and Fish
Undersea volcanoes and waves
All work together in a world of their own
Far underneath the sea

The moon and the gravity guide the tides
Which wash against our shores
Bringing a glimpse of the saltwater world
Which lives beneath the waves.

Reading Rap
Written by fifth graders

Yo—We're the dudes from Mrs. Case's class
We love to read—it's such a blast.
We find our books in libraries
Fiction, literature, biographies.
We do our reports—they're sometimes fun
And we get to use books to get the work done
We read in the classroom, also at home
Even when we're talking on the telephone
We read a book called *Wrinkle in Time*
Everybody liked it . . . now it's hard to find
Reading histories and mysteries
Always enlarges our vocabularies
We like reading—it's in our bones
Especially mysteries like Sherlock Holmes
Thanks to the authors and their good deeds
We now have many great books to read
Now we think our message is clear
Reading is a lot better than sitting here!

Thanks to Robin Case.

Assessment: Demonstrations of Understanding

Student _____ Date _____

Book _____

1. The reader demonstrated understanding through (art, drama, music), or

_____

Observations: _____

_____

		Minimal			Substantial	
1.	The quality of the work was	1	2	3	4	5
2.	The reader's use of reading and/or writing in this response was	1	2	3	4	5
3.	The learner's level of understanding on this topic or text was	1	2	3	4	5
4.	Comments					

Parent Page:
Plan a Story, Write a Story, Make a Book

Please work with your child to use the three circles on this page to plan a story about your family. It can be something that really happened or a story you make up.

Draw a picture in each circle. These will be the illustrations for your story. Encourage your child to talk a lot about the pictures.

Cut out the circles with your pictures inside and glue them onto three blank pages.

Put the pages in order. Write a story to match the pictures on each page.

Add a front and back cover, plus a title. Staple it together and sign your names! Enjoy reading the book to your family and friends.

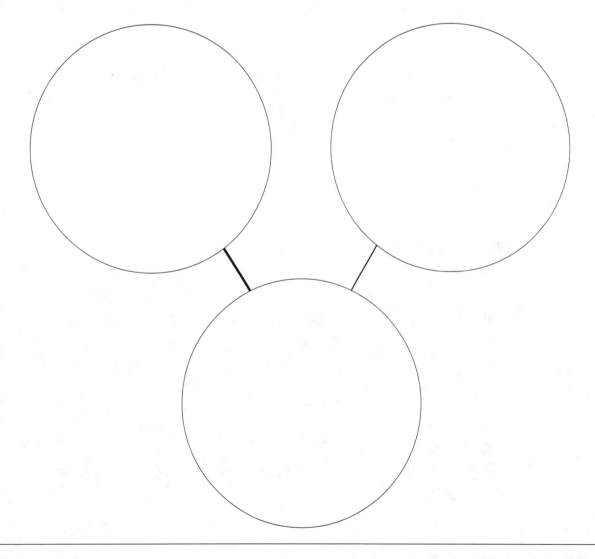

Parent Letter: Drawing to Learn

Dear Parents,

You have been watching your children draw since they were very small. Did you know that drawing is very essential to children's understanding of the world? It helps them organize their thinking and satisfies a need for personal response to the world.

The next time you read to your child, you might think about asking your child to draw a picture about the story you read. It would be even better if you drew a picture, too, and then you and your child could talk about your drawings.

When children draw a picture about a story, they have to think about all of the important parts of a story, then choose the part that seems most interesting. While this may sound simple, it is the essence of reading comprehension—the ability to look at all of the information and pick out the important parts.

When children draw and write about a story or an experience, they learn even more. So, please keep reading and drawing!

Your child's teacher

Epilogue

As I bring closure to this episode in my never ending search for ways to help students expand their competency as readers, I realize that I have a personal need to restate something I said at the opening of this book. Too many students are placed in situations where they do little more than take in words to get through an assignment and comply with teacher directions. They don't get excited about ideas; they aren't actively involved as readers.

The purpose of this book is not to basalize or mechanize the reading process. The purpose is not to lessen the importance of curriculum that is a flexible negotiation between caring teachers and committed learners. The purpose of this book is to offer some kernels of possibility, some soil in which fertile young minds might create newer, better, more personal responses to learning.

As you think about the possibilities, please also think about the following:

Evaluating Student Tasks

1. When I plan instruction, am I asking students to engage in learning that is significant, learning that will shape them as life-long learners?
2. Does the task require higher order thinking?
3. Is the knowledge deep or superficial and shallow?
4. Is the activity connected to the outside world? Is it related to world knowledge or in a format that the learner can use throughout life?
5. Does the task require social engagement and language use?
6. Is this something that students WANT to do?
7. Does this learner NEED a structured response experience or would this learner be better served by more reading?

I wish you and your students a lifetime of reading and the joy that comes from finishing a good book.

Bibliography

Allington, R. 1994. "The Schools We Have. The Schools We Need." *Reading Teacher* 48 (1): 14.

Booth, D. 1987. *Drama Words.* Toronto, ON: University of Toronto.

Braunger, J., and J. Lewis. 1997. *Building a Knowledge Base in Reading.* Urbana, IL: National Council of Teachers of English, and Newark, NJ: International Reading Assocation.

Brown, A. 1986. *The Piggybook.* New York: Knopf.

Brown, H., and B. Cambourne. 1987. *Read and Retell.* Portsmouth, NH: Heinemann.

Calkins, L. 1986. *The Art of Teaching Writing.* Portsmouth, NH: Heinemann.

Cambourne, B. 1995. "Conditions of Learning." *Reading Teacher* 18 (2).

Clay, M. 1972. *Reading: The Patterning of Complex Behavior.* Portsmouth, NH: Heinemann.

Cooper, J. David. 1993. *Literacy: Helping Children Construct Meaning.* Boston: Houghton Mifflin.

Feathers, K. 1993. *Infotext: Reading and Learning.* Ontario: Pippin.

Graves, D. 1982. *Writing: Teachers and Children at Work.* Portsmouth, NH: Heinemann.

Hall, S. 1990. *Using Picture Storybooks to Teach Literary Devices.* Phoenix, AZ: Oryx.

Harste, J., K. Short, and C. Burke. 1988. *Creating Classrooms for Authors.* Portsmouth, NH: Heinemann.

Hill, B., and C. Ruptic. 1994. *Practical Aspects of Authentic Asssessment: Putting the Pieces Together.* Norwood, MA: Christopher-Gordon.

Hoyt, L. 1995. *Accelerating Reading and Writing Success for At Risk Learners.* Bellevue, WA: Bureau of Education and Research.

———. 1992. "Many Ways of Knowing: Using Drama, Oral Interactions, and the Visual Arts to Enhance Reading Comprehension." *Reading Teacher* 45 (8): 580–84.

———. 1990. "Many Ways of Knowing." In *With Promise,* edited by S. Stires. Portsmouth, NH: Heinemann.

———. 1988. "Jazzing Up Reading Through Expressive Arts." In *Literacy in the 90s,* edited by N. Cecil. Dubuque, IA: Kendall/Hunt.

———. 1986. "Tell All About It." *Northwest Reader* 5: 24–9.

Hoyt, L. and C. Ames. 1997. "Letting the Learner Lead the Way." *Primary Voices* 5 (3): 16–29.

Moline, S. 1995. *I See What You Mean.* York, ME: Stenhouse.

Morrow, L. 1996. *Literacy Centers.* York, ME: Stenhouse.

Nash, M. 1997. "Fertile Minds." *Time* (3 February), 48–63.

Peterson, R., and M. Eeds. 1990. *Grand Conversations.* New York: Scholastic.

Routman, R. 1991. *Invitations.* Portsmouth, NH: Heinemann.

Seigel, M. 1984. "Sketch to Stretch." In *Reading, Writing, and Caring,* edited by O. Cochran. New York: Richard C. Owen.

Watson, D. 1987. "Assessment Suggestions for Literature Discussion Groups." In *Ideas and Insights: Language Arts in the Elementary School.* Urbana, IL: National Council of Teachers of English.

Wilson, J. 1997. "Primary Literacy Through Science." Presentation given at the Oregon Reading Association, in Portland, OR, February 16, 1997.

Wilson, R., and J. Cleland. 1985. *Diagnostic and Remedial Reading for Classroom and Clinic.* Columbus, OH: Merrill.